DEVIL'S ADVOCATE

Facing My Inner Anti-Catholic

TRENT HORN

Catholic
Answers
Press

Published by
Catholic Answers, Inc.
2020 Gillespie Way
El Cajon, California 92020
1-888-291-8000 orders
619-387-0042 fax
catholic.com

Printed in the United States of America

Cover design by Theodore Schluenderfritz
Interior design by Claudine Mansour Design

978-1-68357-278-7
978-1-68357-279-4 Kindle
978-1-68357-280-0 ePub

Contents

DIFFICULTIES WITH MORAL TEACHINGS

Introduction

There was one book C.S. Lewis said he didn't enjoy writing. After finishing this book, I know how he felt.

In 1942, Lewis published *The Screwtape Letters*, which consists of a series of letters from Screwtape, an experienced demon, to his incompetent, inexperienced nephew, Wormwood, who is learning how to tempt people. The book is one of Lewis's most popular, due in part to the uniqueness of its primary literary device. Instead of writing yet another book on how to avoid temptation, Lewis lets us "peer behind enemy lines" so we see the traps the evil one lays for us and respond accordingly.

In a 1963 interview, Lewis confessed that *The Screwtape Letters* was his least favorite book. He said,

> Of all my books, there was only one I did not take pleasure in writing: *The Screwtape Letters*. They were dry and gritty going. At the time, I was thinking of objections to the Christian life, and decided to put them into the form, "That's what the devil would say." But making goods "bad" and bads "good" gets to be fatiguing.[1]

In this book, I feel a similar strain—but fortunately, I didn't have to come up with snappy demonic quips. One of the voices is friendly and familiar because he's me, but the other voice is also friendly (if a bit cheeky) and familiar. That's what makes him terrifying: he's the voice of doubt—a real one, voicing real doubts—deep inside me. I suspect most people who read this book have had conversations with this same sort of person when they finally have some time to be alone with their thoughts. It may even be comforting to know that saints and Doctors of the Church (as well as your friendly neighborhood apologist) have doubts, so there's nothing wrong with you having them, too.

My goal in this book is to share how I've engaged this persistent adversary. I can't teach you how to answer your own specific "inner skeptic," because I've never met that person. People are unique, so what might be an insurmountable objection to one person will be just another apologetics trivia question for another. But if I show you as honestly as possible how I handle my own doubts, through a dialogue between myself and my "devil's advocate," then hopefully you'll come away from this book with a rough plan of attack to face the challenges to the Catholic faith that hit you the hardest.

Before you write off the concept of a devil's advocate, keep in mind that it was the Catholic Church who came up with the term. The office arose in the Middle Ages as the process of canonizing saints became reserved exclusively to the Holy See. In 1587, Pope Sixtus V established the office of the *Promoter of the Faith*, whose job was to ensure that candidates for sainthood really had exhibited the holiness others claimed for them and that the miracles attributed to them were authentic. Sixtus's promoter became popularly known as the *advocatus diaboli*, the devil's advocate, who tried to disprove the causes put forward by the *advocatus dei*, or the "promoter of the cause." After the revision of the Code of Canon Law in 1983, Pope St. John Paul II reduced the role of the devil's advocate, but his essential purpose is still carried out in Vatican investigations of those being beatified or canonized. (In 2003, atheist Christopher Hitchens volunteered to be the devil's advocate against Mother Teresa's beatification. That's . . . not exactly how it works, but points to Hitchens for his enthusiasm.)

The Church saw fit to assign someone the role of attempting to shoot down canonizations to show that seeking strong evidence against your own position isn't a bad thing. For example, showing that one argument for the Faith isn't any good may be an opportunity to replace it with a much stronger argument. But that doesn't mean it's easy to examine your beliefs in this way. Oftentimes, it can feel like writing dialogue for demons: uncomfortable, unnerving, and even spiritually grimy. But if this can help people see that 1) it is normal to have doubts and 2) there are practical steps we can take to address them and strengthen our faith in the process, then it will be well worth the discomfort.

Having published nine books now over a decade-long apologetics career, I'm late to the game when it comes to writing dialogues. But that's not to say I don't appreciate the genre. In fact, some of my favorite apologetics books have been dialogues, especially those of Peter Kreeft. In an essay I wrote about Kreeft in the anthology *Wisdom and Wonder: How Peter Kreeft Shaped the Next Generation of Catholics*, I said,

> It would be easy for a philosopher to turn a philosophical essay into a mediocre dialogue by just putting the arguments for his position in a character's mouth and the rebuttals and counterarguments into the mouth of another character. Kreeft, however, adds little details to the narrative, and this makes his works all the more fun to read. For example, before the next set of dialogues [in *The Unaborted Socrates*], the other characters marvel that Socrates is now wearing a business suit to the Athenian convention of philosophers.

The challenge in writing dialogue books is that it's hard to craft a worthy skeptical antagonist when you, the author, "hold all the cards." I made a point of tackling this problem head-on, right after you finish reading this introduction, and I'm pleased to announce that it turns out only a little awkward.

It would have been a lot more awkward if not for my friend Randal Rauser, to whom I owe a debt of gratitude, and his book *Conversations with My Inner Atheist: A Christian Apologist Explores Questions that Keep People Up at Night*. Randal is a Protestant theologian, so there is a fair amount we disagree about, including which doubts about the Faith are most concerning. But we agree that it's important to treat our interlocutors with charity (especially when "they" are ourselves!) and not to settle for pat answers to difficult problems. For example, Randal's interlocutor often points out when answers are unsatisfying, and Randal is quick to admit when he doesn't quite know how to resolve a difficult issue.

After I read *Conversations with My Inner Atheist*, I told Randal I thought it was a fun book. "Maybe I should write one," I said, and he replied, "You definitely should." And so here we are . . . and here you are, too, to sit in on a conversation that may be unusual and yet all too familiar to you.

CHAPTER 1

A Used-Faith Salesman

DAVID: Why are you doing this?

TRENT: Doing what?

DAVID: This. This whole "I'm going to write a book where I talk to my 'inner skeptic' about my doubts" thing.

TRENT: Well, it's an interesting idea, and people can see how I investigate my concerns with the Catholic faith.

DAVID: But it's not really an *honest* investigation, is it?

TRENT: What do you mean?

DAVID: Look. You're the equivalent of a used-car salesman. A "used-faith salesman," if you will. This book isn't about honestly wrestling with doubts that could lead to you abandoning the Faith. This is about you glossing over the car's problems in order to dupe some sucker into buying it. Why should anyone trust your opinion of Catholicism when you're so biased in favor of it?

TRENT: Let's pump the brakes on your analogy—and you can just trust me that the brakes work fine. In your example, the salesman knows the car is a lemon and is practicing deception. I sincerely believe that the Catholic faith is true, good, and beautiful. I could be sincerely wrong, but I'm not trying to sell anyone a faulty product.

DAVID: Really? How much is this book going for online?

TRENT: The fact that you can purchase this book, or Richard Dawkins's *The God Delusion*, or any other book doesn't mean the author is only out to make money. Also, pointing out that someone has made money selling a book does nothing to disprove the arguments in that book.

Ad Hominem Argument

A fallacy, or error in reasoning, that tries to refute an argument by attacking the person making it (such as by saying he's only out to make money). Even if David were right about Trent only being interested in making money from book sales, that would not refute any of Trent's arguments. An argument's strength is not affected by the person making it.

DAVID: But if you're convinced Catholicism is true, then why do you still have doubts?

TRENT: I don't have "doubts" if by doubts you mean I formally reject something the Church obligates me to believe. I admit, some things the Church teaches are difficult, but every belief system has difficulties. I've read atheists who think consciousness and objective morality must be illusions because they are so difficult to explain apart from God.[2] I've read Protestants who admit that some Bible passages seem to support what they consider "unbiblical" Catholic doctrine.[3]

Difficulties are a bad reason to reject a worldview, because all worldviews have some.

DAVID: Right, but you think those difficulties can't be overcome, and so those critics should become Catholic. Isn't it hypocritical for you not to convert in the face of similar difficulties with Catholicism?

TRENT: Well, I don't think the difficulties are *similar* in the sense that they are equally difficult, even if all of them may seem insurmountable at first glance. Not every case offered by an "apologist" will be equally sound. For example, some atheists I've spoken to have said Muslim apologetics is inferior to Christian apologetics and that, of all the Christian denominations, Catholicism has one of the most robust theological defenses.[4] Also, the fact that every belief system has difficulties doesn't mean every belief system is false. Some of them have to be right, at least about some things.

The evidence for different religions is not equal. Some could be more reasonable than others.

Apologetics

A defense of a particular position. In Catholicism, it is a branch of theology dedicated to providing a rational defense of the Christian faith. Trent says all religions do not have equally compelling apologetics.

DAVID: Why can't they all be wrong?

"Ten thousand difficulties do not make one doubt."
—St. John Henry Newman

TRENT: Because sometimes they disagree on fundamental "either/or" questions. For example, either atheists are right, and God doesn't exist, or theists are right, and God does exist. Either Christians are right, and Jesus rose from the dead, or non-Christians are right, and he didn't. In those cases, there is no third option. And, after reviewing the evidence, I believe that Catholicism has the greatest chance of being true in spite of some of its difficulties.

DAVID: Yeah, but you make a *living* defending the Catholic faith. There is no way you are going to write a book that cancels your meal ticket.

TRENT: Are you implying that I would keep doing apologetics even if I lost my faith?

DAVID: I'm just saying you care about providing for your family. I mean, if you were really honest and Catholicism turned out to not be true, then you'd have to give up your job, your livelihood. Would you really do that?

TRENT: I'd have to. I hear stories from Protestant pastors who gave up their careers to become Catholic. If I would encourage that kind of sacrifice in the pursuit of truth, then I'd have to be willing to do the same. Besides, I'm sure I could find some other career, given the weird things I talk about on the free-for-all Friday segments of my podcast. (I'd better buy the URL to trenthorndisasterprep.com!)

DAVID: But this book is going to be so boring. We all know how it's going to end. I make the objections, and then you, the apologist, the defender of the Faith, ride in with all the perfect answers. And since you control what I'm saying, it's not going to be a fair fight. You can always make sure you win, so why would anyone even bother reading this?

Would you give up everything to follow the truth?

Straw Man

A fallacy that occurs when an argument is misrepresented to make it weaker and, as a result, easier to refute. David is concerned that Trent will make a straw man of the critical arguments against Catholicism.

Can an apologist create a convincing critic?

TRENT: Because I don't have the perfect answer to every question.

DAVID: Well, that's refreshing!

TRENT: For example, in the face of some difficulties, there may be different possible answers, and I haven't decided which is the most likely answer. And you're right: I am biased. But so are you. So is everyone. Let's not pretend there is some group of people who are immune to bias that can settle these questions for us. We all have psychological defects that lead us to confirmation bias, or the tendency to welcome evidence that supports our beliefs and ignore evidence that contradicts those beliefs. That's why I'm excited to write this book with you, David.

DAVID: Me? Why?

TRENT: Because you ask those questions that keep me

from accepting easy answers that may not be true. So go ahead. Let's have an honest talk about some tough issues. Besides, since I'm the author, you don't really have much of a choice in the matter!

DAVID: All right. Let's have a chat, then, and see how tight I can pull these "strings you've got on me."

Our inner skeptic keeps us from accepting easy but flawed answers.

CHAPTER 2

Why Not Heaven Now?

DAVID: All right, let's start with a subject that is probably the most difficult of them all: the problem of evil.

TRENT: I've written and spoken about this one a lot, but go ahead.

> Why did God create a world with so much evil and suffering?

DAVID: Obviously you've got the well standard, well-worn answers. Moral evil makes sense, in some cases, because it's better to have humans who do evil instead of humans who are mindless robots without free will.

The Problem of Evil

An argument for atheism that claims that the existence of evil or suffering makes the existence of an all-good, all-powerful God incredibly unlikely or even impossible.

TRENT: Agreed.

Why can't God take a world without evil (heaven) and make it now?

"Why is there evil?" is not an argument for atheism; it's a question everyone should investigate.

DAVID: But when we're in heaven, we won't be evil, and we won't be robots. Why doesn't God just make heaven now and skip all this nonsense on earth?

TRENT: Notice that this is a question—it's not an argument. I could say "I don't know," and there still wouldn't be a reason for me to doubt the Catholic faith.

DAVID: Fine, here's an argument, then: if God is all-good, then he should do the most good he can. But if that were true, then why would God make this world? Surely he could make something better than this! If he can make heaven, then surely he can make heaven *right now*.

TRENT: First, don't call me Shirley. Second, here's a question for you: could God make a world better than heaven?

DAVID: No, heaven is the best world God could make.

TRENT: Okay, that's the problem with your argument. You're assuming there is a "best of all possible worlds" or some world with "maximal goodness." But that kind of world doesn't exist.

DAVID: How do you know that?

TRENT: Because that'd be like saying God can make the "best island" or "the largest number."

DAVID: Infinity is the largest number.

TRENT: Infinity isn't a number! It's a way of communicating a lack of limits. But there is no number you could write out that is "the largest number," since you can always add something to it.

DAVID: I'm guessing you don't believe in perfect islands, either?

TRENT: What is "the best island"? God could always make a better island by adding one more luau or one more pair of coconut trees, so there is no "best island," just like there is no "largest number." Likewise, there is no "best of all possible worlds." God could always make a "better world" than the one he creates. That's why you can't fault God for making a world that is "less good" than some world he didn't create, since there will always be a world like that.

> "God freely willed to create a world 'in a state of journeying' toward its ultimate perfection" (CCC 310).

Best of All Possible Worlds

A philosophical idea about a kind of world God could create that has maximal perfection or goodness. Trent says no such world could ever exist because there is no upper limit to good things that could be added to such a world.

DAVID: I disagree. What if God made something like heaven but with an infinite number of souls that enjoy infinite happiness? It can't get any better than that.

TRENT: Even St. Thomas Aquinas, who thought God could make a world with an infinite past, did not think God could make a world with an infinite number of things in it since that creates contradictions.[5] But I'll set that aside because even if your example were possible, God could still make a world with more goodness in it.

DAVID: How? What goodness could a world with infinite happiness be missing?

TRENT: You're thinking of *goodness* as being just about one kind of thing. To you, goodness is just one kind of "premium fuel" that God uses to fill up the world's tank. But goodness is more like a series of jewels: just as there are different jewels (emeralds, diamonds, rubies), there are different goods, and some of them conflict with one another. For example, what about the good that happens when someone reconciles with an enemy who's wronged him? Or the good of risking your life in order to protect someone in danger? Those goods can exist only alongside evils like hatred and harm. In the world you want God to create, there couldn't be goods like compassion, courage, mercy, patience, sacrifice, and forgiveness.

DAVID: But are those things really worth it if we can have infinite happiness instead?

TRENT: Yes, I think they are worth it. We aren't God's pets or mere bodies in "the Matrix" that God tries to keep as happy as possible. We have more dignity than that. Also, when it comes to having either goods that accompany suffering or infinite happiness, I would quote the little girl from the Old El Paso at-home taco kit commercial: why not both?

DAVID: I don't see how infinite happiness could ever include any amount of suffering.

TRENT: Well, what's infinity plus any finite negative number?

DAVID: I get it. Infinity. You're saying that no matter how much unhappiness we endure in this life, the total

A world with infinite happiness would be lacking other goods that exist alongside evil.

Are goods that exist with evil worth the evil they need for their existence?

amount of happiness we will have if we go to heaven is still infinite.

TRENT: I would say the math checks out.

DAVID: Great. So it doesn't matter if a twelve-year-old-girl gets kidnapped and raped in some maniac's sex dungeon because she can go to heaven and still have infinite happiness.

TRENT: That's not what I said.

DAVID: But it's what you meant.

TRENT: What do you want me to say? This girl suffers, dies in this monster's basement, he never gets caught, and then this creep disappears into the void of death and never pays for his crimes? Stories like that make me want to throw up.

DAVID: Hey, go complain to the Manager if you don't like it.

Moral Facts

Also called *objective moral truths* or *objective moral values and duties*, these are rules about how persons ought to act that are objective—not dependent on changing personal or societal conventions.

TRENT: Obviously, these evils matter. I never said they didn't. And I understand being mad at God when you hear about them. But when I hear about grotesque evils, it also convicts me to believe, without a doubt, that moral facts like *rape is always wrong* are sewn into

"This slight momentary affliction is preparing for us an eternal weight of glory beyond all comparison" (2 Cor. 4:17).

God can give you infinite happiness in heaven, and this will always infinitely outweigh any harms you experienced on earth.

the fabric of the universe. And that doesn't make sense unless something, or *someone*, did the sewing.

DAVID: Fine. Maybe God can allow evils to happen to human beings and compensate them with heaven, but there are still two other problems you have to deal with: animal suffering and hell.

TRENT: I'm guessing you aren't worried about animals going to hell.

DAVID: Quite the opposite. The traditional teaching of theologians is that animals don't go to heaven. And some animals in this life experience horrendous suffering. Think about a deer trapped in a forest fire or a water buffalo being devoured from the inside by flesh-eating parasites. What good reason does God have for allowing these animals to suffer, especially for millions of years before humans ever evolved?

TRENT: That one is harder, and I don't know the exact answer.

DAVID: Gotcha!

TRENT: But . . . if God has good reasons for allowing humans to suffer *and* if he's all-powerful and all-knowing, then it would be foolish for me to say God could not possibly have any reasons for allowing non-human animals to suffer.

DAVID: Sounds like the old "God is a mystery" cop-out.

TRENT: Not at all. We should be humble and admit that we aren't in a good position to know all the reasons

Some moral evils are so repugnant that they clearly reveal the existence of a universal moral law.

Do animals go to heaven?

God has for allowing any particular evil to occur. But I can think of some plausible reasons for why God would allow animal suffering.

Skeptical Theism

An approach to the problem of evil that stresses the inability of fallible, finite human beings to know the specific reason God allows certain evils to exist. This means human beings are not justified in saying such reasons do not exist.

CHAPTER 3

Red in Tooth and Claw

DAVID: This isn't a Disney movie. Animals can't experience goods like forgiveness or courage, so why even create them at all? What good reasons could God have for allowing animals to suffer?

TRENT: Animals can experience some goods even if they aren't *higher-order* goods like forgiveness. Some, like most mammals, can experience pleasure from sunshine, food, and sleep.

Higher-Order Goods

Some goods are universal for created things, like the good of existing. Other goods are shared by only some things, like the good of organic growth in living beings. David is saying animals cannot access the highest goods, or personal virtues, that Christians use to justify God allowing evil to exist.

DAVID: But the pleasure these animals experience is so small compared to the pains, even moderate ones, they experience on a daily basis.

TRENT: But if you made a world with animals that didn't feel pain, they wouldn't really be animals. They wouldn't have instincts that drive them to behave as animals do in the presence of pain. They'd just be robots.

DAVID: Not necessarily. God could make it so that when an animal "needs to die" to balance the ecosystem, it just painlessly drops dead.

Are animals that aren't aware of their surroundings an impossibility that God can't create, like a square circle?

TRENT: I'm skeptical that God could create a world like that and have it still be natural, or operate according to fixed laws instead of being something that's just one miracle after another.

DAVID: Well, what's wrong with a miraculous world without suffering?

TRENT: What's wrong is that we might be losing more things than just the suffering. There are many good things you might not have in such a world. I'd also ask: what's wrong with creating creatures that can suffer?

DAVID: Well, suffering is bad, Einstein! God should eliminate suffering whenever he can.

TRENT: Maybe God wanted human beings to be connected to other creatures so that, through mankind's redemption in Christ, all of creation would eventually be redeemed.

DAVID: Not buying it. God could have made humans

from nothing, or from the "dust of the earth." He didn't need to require creatures to suffer for millennia when we weren't even on the planet. And we didn't need to evolve from them.

"The creation itself will be set free from its bondage to decay and obtain the glorious liberty of the children of God" (Rom. 8:21).

TRENT: I agree that we didn't need to evolve from lower animals, and the Church does allow us to believe that we did not evolve from them.

DAVID: Of course, but that would be at the cost of what science tells us about the origin of life. And even if it's true that we didn't evolve from lower animals, blaming Adam and Eve for animal suffering still means God allowed thousands of years of animal suffering that didn't have to happen, either. There's no need for him to punish them for our mistakes. Either way, an all-good God should eliminate suffering whenever he can.

If animal suffering is so bad, should we destroy all animals?

TRENT: I agree. God shouldn't cause suffering just for the sake of inflicting pain in the absence of any good reason. And I have a thought experiment that helps show why such a reason to justify animal suffering probably exists.

DAVID: All right. Let's have it.

TRENT: Okay, suppose we were exploring the universe in a futuristic starship, and we came across a planet like earth, except there were no humans. There were just non-human animals like lions and zebras. And let's further imagine that our ship has a device that lets you vaporize a planet—just wipe it out of existence in the blink of an eye. Now, here's my question: would you wipe this planet out of existence in order to reduce animal suffering?

Anti-natalism

The view that life is not worth living, so it is wrong to bring creatures, especially humans, into existence. Some atheists believe that God's nonexistence entails anti-natalism, whereas other atheists deny anti-natalism. If atheism did logically demand anti-natalism, then confidence in the falsehood of anti-natalism would be powerful evidence for the existence of God.

If humans can have good reasons to tolerate animal suffering, then how do we know an infinite God lacks similar reasons?

DAVID: I'm not sure. But I think there is a difference between creating animals capable of feeling pain when you didn't have to create them and allowing animals that can feel pain to continue to exist.

TRENT: But what's the difference? I thought a good person "eliminates evil as much as he can." If we followed that advice, it would seem as if a good person would vaporize this planet in order to prevent the evil of animal suffering. But your hesitance shows that the existence of animals that feel pain, even large amounts of it, contains enough goodness to justify their existence. That counts against animal suffering being an unjustifiable part of God's creation.

DAVID: By that logic, if I had a button and you pushed it and animal suffering decreased by fifty percent, would you push the button? If you would, then why doesn't God do the same thing and reduce animal suffering?

TRENT: Your example isn't like mine because it's way less specific. How does the button cut animal suffering in half? Does it cause half of all animals to disappear? Does it dull animal sensation by fifty percent and make them "half-robots"? The more I get specifics, the more I'm inclined not to push the button, but the same isn't true for my scenario.

Can animals go to heaven?

DAVID: Maybe, but your thought experiment doesn't neatly do away with the problem, either.

If animals lack awareness to make them capable of perceiving heaven, then they won't be as aware of suffering.

TRENT: No single explanation really does for the problem of evil. But another thing that might help us understand why God allows animal suffering is the possibility that God could compensate animals in the afterlife.

DAVID: You're really going to play the "all dogs go to heaven" card?

TRENT: At least for dogs; I'm not so sure about cats.

DAVID: Most theologians say animals don't have immortal souls, so they can't go to heaven. Animals don't experience themselves as conscious individuals over time, so they aren't the kind of being that could.

TRENT: Animals probably wouldn't behold the beatific vision, or be in heaven, but perhaps they will be given unending natural happiness, like what some past theologians proposed for unbaptized children in limbo.

And that leaves us with two interesting options. First, if animals don't experience a conscious awareness of suffering over time, then the problem of animal suffering isn't so problematic. Animals just may not have an awareness of being in pain like what you and I have since they don't have a conscious awareness of themselves (or an *I*) that exists over time.[6] But if they are consciously aware of themselves over time, even in a rudimentary way, then God could alleviate their overall suffering in the afterlife just as he does with human beings.

DAVID: This all sounds very convenient to me. Let's try looking at this with objective probabilities. If atheism or naturalism is true, and God doesn't exist, then we'd expect the world to look like this. We'd expect lots of gratuitous pain from an unconscious creative process like biological evolution. But if God does exist, then this kind of pain and suffering is very unlikely. I'm just saying the world looks an awful lot as though God doesn't exist.

If God didn't exist, a painful process like evolution is what we'd expect.

TRENT: I'm skeptical of these kinds of probability arguments for atheism because they often contain a double standard regarding the assumptions that go into them.

DAVID: What do you mean?

TRENT: Well, I could easily say that if God did not exist, we would expect there to be no world at all, or at least a very chaotic one that doesn't have complex life forms. So, from my perspective, the world looks an awful lot as though God does exist.

Anthropic Principle

The observation that any speculation about the nature of the universe will only take place in a universe containing intelligent life. Trent thinks arguments that assume that the universe would always have intelligent life in it even if God did not exist take the existence of that life for granted.

DAVID: But maybe there are things about the universe we don't understand that explain why it's not unlikely that the universe would exist and even have intelligent life evolve in it.

TRENT: That's it! That's the double-standard!

DAVID: I beg your pardon?

If atheists believe that unknown scientific explanations for natural phenomena could exist, then they should believe that unknown theological explanations for evil phenomena could exist.

TRENT: You're willing to accept that the universe is "mysterious," and so it may contain explanations for things you don't understand, like how an improbably life-permitting universe could come into existence for no reason. But you also say it's a cop-out to claim that God is mysterious and may have explanations for things we don't understand, like the presence of seemingly gratuitous evils.

DAVID: Then let us be at a standstill: suffering in the universe doesn't prove there is no God, but complexity in the universe doesn't prove there is a God. The mystery destroys theism and atheism equally, leaving us with good old-fashioned agnosticism.

The evidence for God from the moral duty toward animals outweighs evidence against God found in animal suffering.

TRENT: Not so fast. There is one thing about animal suffering that points me toward God and away from atheism: I have a moral duty to be kind to non-human animals.

DAVID: Atheists can explain our moral duties toward animals. It simply comes from our general moral duty not to cause unnecessary pain, no matter who or what is in pain.

TRENT: But that pushes the problem back one step: where does that moral duty come from?

DAVID: Evolution. We evolved the ability as human beings to be empathetic toward one another. Tribes with people who were empathetic did better than tribes that weren't, and we are their "touchy-feely" descendants who managed to survive.

TRENT: But how do you get a "duty" from this story? I agree that evolution explains our moral feelings. It explains why we are scared of spiders that kill few people and why we love fast food that kills many people (over time, at least). But duties can come from only persons, not processes.

Also, we have moral duties beyond not just causing unnecessary pain. Let me ask you a question: what is evil?

Evolution explains why humans should be kind to non-human animals.

A natural process can't give me a duty to act in a certain way.

DAVID: I prefer to talk about unnecessary suffering because it's a more concrete concept than evil.

TRENT: And that's what gives me doubts about atheism. I've had many atheists say evil is a *basic* or a *redundant* concept that's not even worth defining. But I know evil when I see it. The man who casually tears the wings off a fly, destroys beautiful flowers just to see them burn, or fantasizes about raping children (even if he never acts on those thoughts) is evil. It may be a simplistic definition, but something is evil when it is not the way it is supposed to be, and something is good when it is supposed to be a certain way, and is that way. And for me, if the world exhibits "supposed to be" qualities, that is at least a signpost that points to a perfect creator.

Defining "evil" is problematic for atheists.

DAVID: Except I can throw a monkey wrench into your whole scheme with one thing this "perfect creator," if he's the Christian God, did create and doesn't seem as though it's *supposed to be* that way . . .

Evil happens when things in creation are not the way they are supposed to be.

Evil

An absence of good or being. Occurs when a thing lacks something it ought to have. Evil can be non-moral, like a "bad tree" that doesn't produce fruit, or moral, like a bad person who steals fruit for fun.

CHAPTER 4

A Hell of a Problem

DAVID: So far, most of your responses to the problem of evil have relied on God being able to make everything well in the end. The rape victim and maybe even the deer trapped in a forest fire both go to heaven. Everything works out in "God's grand scheme of things."

TRENT: That's a part of my response to the problem of evil. But I do think God will balance the scales. And, since he's all-knowing, all-good, and all-powerful, he will right every wrong.

DAVID: Not for people in hell. It sounds as if there will be unending tears and pain for them. That seems to be the Achilles heel of your argument: it's one kind of evil that will never go away. It's something that makes you scream, "That's not the way it's supposed to be!"

TRENT: I agree that people rejecting God is evil or

something that's "not supposed to be," but allowing those people to exist in hell doesn't fall under the same category of evil because hell is an appropriate response to someone who rejects God.

Does hell contradict the existence of a perfectly good God?

DAVID: Sure, because whenever someone rejects my friendship, I throw him into an unquenchable barbeque . . .

Rejecting the traditional doctrine of hell doesn't require rejecting God.

TRENT: I understand that this is a difficult subject, so right at the outset, I would tell a critic that rejecting the classical view of hell doesn't require him to become an atheist. You could believe in God and also think everyone is going to heaven. Or you could be an *annihilationist*, who thinks the damned are destroyed and do not consciously experience hell forever.

Universalism

The belief that all human beings, and possibly all creatures, will eventually spend eternity with God in heaven, leaving hell empty. The Church condemned this as a heresy at the Council of Orange in 529.

DAVID: But you've argued against both of these positions in your books and podcasts. You've even said the odds of universalism being true are on par with winning the lottery, so it's nothing you'd bet your life on.

TRENT: True, I'm neither an annihilationist nor a universalist, but you could be a theist and not believe in an unending hell for the damned. That being said, if the unrepentant serial rapist you talked about in our previous exchange is in hell, I won't be shedding any tears over that.

DAVID: I thought we were supposed to love our enemies, not be indifferent toward their eternal torture!

TRENT: I admit I'm letting my emotions get the best of me here, and I probably shouldn't do that. But sometimes, in these discussions about hell, we just think of the damned as our friends who got lazy about going to church and are now being dragged kicking and screaming into hell. We shouldn't gloat over someone being damned, but it's also not wrong to feel good when God "makes things right" and restores justice.

DAVID: But how could it be just for someone to receive an infinite punishment for a finite crime? Even something as terrible as running a sex dungeon for decades doesn't merit infinite punishment in hell.

TRENT: I hear about *infinite punishment* a lot when talking about hell, but something about the idea seems off to me. Punishment isn't something that can be measured in a unit like pounds or degrees. There is no *thing* that contains an infinite amount of punishment that the damned are given in hell. Hell is just a punishment that never ends. And if that's true, then we should ask: "Could there ever be a crime that justifies an unending punishment?"

DAVID: No. There is no crime that would justify a zillion years of punishment.

TRENT: A zillion isn't a real number.

The damned are not just people who have differences of opinions with Christians.

Is it true that people are punished infinitely in hell? Do some crimes merit unending punishment?

DAVID: You know what I mean.

TRENT: What about an unending crime? If there were a crime that never ended, then it would make sense that the punishment would never end, either. This has helped me come to grips with the fairness of the traditional doctrine of hell. You see, when we look around the world, it's easy to see slight degrees in goodness among people, even non-religious people.

Annihilationism

The belief that God destroys the damned after the Final Judgment and so they do not have eternal, conscious existence in hell. While not formally condemned as a heresy, the vast majority of Catholic tradition opposes this view of hell.

DAVID: Exactly. There are some virtuous atheists who seem better fit for heaven than some so-called "Christians."

TRENT: And it may be the case God will mercifully give eternal life to the blamelessly ignorant while he tells unrepentant, evil Christians, "I never knew you; depart from me, you evildoers" (Matt. 7:23). But my point is that in this life, God sustains everyone, believer and unbeliever, with natural dispositions toward the good. However, at the end of the world, when everything is "laid bare" (2 Pet. 3:10), we will see people's true natures. Do you know what my favorite disaster movies are?

DAVID: The ones where lots of things gratuitously explode, especially famous landmarks?

TRENT: Partially, but I really enjoy disaster movies that show how, in the face of death, ordinary people turn into either heroes or selfish villains. They may seem like nice people at the beginning of the movie, but when the meteor is about to hit, they will bury a clawhammer into your skull in order to get inside the underground bunker for survival. They will do anything to save themselves because their life is really all that matters to them—even if they can put up a good face for other people when things are normal.

DAVID: So you're saying atheists are just a bunch of repressed serial killers?

TRENT: Some atheists, yes. But some Christians, too. What I'm saying is that at the Final Judgment, when we all stand before God, there won't be nice, indifferent people. You'll either have God's grace (whether you know it or not), and so you will love and desire God, or you won't have God's grace or even the natural disposition to do good. As a result, you will hate God and love yourself above all else. To put it bluntly, if you took the damned out of hell and dropped them into heaven, they would march their smoking husks back to hell, all while giving God a one-finger salute.

DAVID: That doesn't give God the right to roast people alive for all eternity just because they have an attitude problem. If a human being did that, we'd rightly consider him a moral monster.

TRENT: Now, when I talk about the fires of hell, I'm referring to a common metaphor. We shouldn't . . .

At the Final Judgment, you will be either with God or against God.

Why is God allowed to do what humans can't?

DAVID: Yeah, yeah, we shouldn't take it *literally*. The fire of hell is a metaphor, blah, blah, blah, it represents being separated from God . . . look, you may try to dress it up, but it's still terrible.

Think about solitary confinement in prison. This punishment drives people insane, and some people are campaigning to end it, just as they do for other human rights abuses. Now, imagine solitary confinement lasting *forever* as hell's chief punishment. You don't need fire to torture people: God can torture people by just leaving them alone for all eternity simply because they've rejected him. How can you ever justify that?

> Even if hell isn't full of fire, is it still cruel and unjust?

> Is hell a punishment for or merely a consequence of rejecting God? Is it both?

TRENT: Let me try to pin down where we disagree: you think that God tortures people because they reject him. However, I think the act of rejecting God *is* the torture that the damned endure. I can see how hell would be unjust if it were an arbitrary punishment God imposed on the damned because he's annoyed that they don't worship him. But if the punishment of hell is *intrinsically* connected to the crime of rejecting God, or if it is a natural consequence of that rejection, then it's not unfair.

DAVID: It would be unfair if God lets us do something so mind-bogglingly stupid like reject him for all eternity. If someone were about to jump off a bridge, you wouldn't "respect his freedom" and let him jump. I bet you'd pull him off the bridge and get him help. God should do the same thing with us when we think of jumping into hell.

TRENT: We need to be careful with analogies between God and human beings. *I* would forcibly keep someone from jumping off a bridge because God has given humans like me a moral duty to help the suicidal. But let's say a person wants to commit suicide because he's read modern philosophers who've convinced him life isn't worth living.[7] If I couldn't convince him those philosophers were wrong, should I strap this guy into a chair à la *Clockwork Orange* and scramble his brain until he thinks life is worth living?

DAVID: I get it. I get it. You're saying you would respect someone's freedom to hold destructive beliefs and not lobotomize him.

TRENT: Consider the movie *Beautiful Boy*, which is based on the true story of David Sheff's battle to save his son from addiction to methamphetamines. At one point in the film, Nic calls his dad and asks to come home, but his father knows that his son hasn't left his addiction behind. If Nic comes home an addict, the destructive process will start all over again. So instead of forcing him into treatment, or imprisoning him at home, David tells his son he *can't* come home.

DAVID: I don't know the lesson you're trying to find in this, since Nic ended up overdosing after that phone call and nearly died.

TRENT: But it was only after that moment, only when Nic was at his lowest, that he saw what he needed to do to turn his life around and come home clean.

My point is that this is a better analogy to God's relationship with us than the suicidal jumper. God is a father who loves his children, but he also respects our freedom.

DAVID: But if Nic did die, then you could say his father

If we wouldn't let people commit physical suicide, why does God let people commit spiritual suicide?

Should we force people to love God? Is forced love even love?

Can God still embrace us in hell?

failed, much like how anyone who goes to hell represents a failure of "our Father in heaven."

TRENT: The analogy will break down somewhat, but not entirely. First, if an adult child is free to make a decision that results in his death, that doesn't mean his parent was negligent. Some adults engage in dangerous activities, like mountain-climbing without a rope, but we wouldn't blame the parents who didn't keep their thirty-year-old grounded for life.

There is also a view of hell that intrigues me—one that can affirm the idea of God allowing us to be free without totally abandoning us.

CHAPTER 5

Why Does God Create the Damned?

DAVID: All right, how does God damn his children without abandoning them?

TRENT: There's a view found in the Eastern Church that says hell is the presence of God for those who hate God. Under this view, everyone in the afterlife experiences God, but those who love sin more than God find God's love and goodness unbearable. It's torture for them. To give you an example, if my hands are warm and yours are warm, then when I hold your hands, it feels pleasant.

DAVID: I'll entertain your Beatles theology.

TRENT: But if your hands were ice-cold, then my warm hands might feel unbearably hot and painful. Here's

31

If hell is
separation
from God,
how could
the damned
grieve his
presence in
hell?

how one Eastern Orthodox priest describes it: "Those who have selfless love and are friends of God see God in light—divine light, while the selfish and impure see God the judge as fire—darkness."[8]

DAVID: I don't know how you would square that with what the *Catechism* says on hell: "The chief punishment of hell is eternal separation from God, in whom alone man can possess the life and happiness for which he was created and for which he longs" (1035). If you still perceive God, even in a painful way, then how would you be separated from him?

TRENT: I think we need a clear definition of what we mean by *separated*. First, there is no way for someone to be *completely* separated from God. God sustains our existence, so people in hell will be united with God in the sense that God will keep them from going out of existence. Second, one could interpret the separation as being a separation from God's friendship or grace. The damned behold God, but they don't behold him as a friend or savior. They see God as a holy judge and a source of goodness they detest with all their being. So the separation is relational, not metaphysical.

DAVID: Eh, it's still endless suffering even if it's the "sinner's fault" for not being able to receive God. If I smelled horrible and were causing someone pain, I'd excuse myself not to burden him. I don't see how God can't be blamed in a similar way for causing torment to sinners by his mere presence.

TRENT: Because there is nothing wrong with God.

Being in a state of finding God painful is completely the fault of the sinner who rejects God.

DAVID: Getting a little feisty, aren't we? You're sounding more like a cocksure Calvinist than a hair-splitting, logic-chopping Catholic apologist.

TRENT: I'm just trying to get at the heart of the matter, which sometimes you need to do in order to find some peace with a doctrine as disturbing as eternal punishment in hell.

DAVID: But how could you be happy in heaven if your loved one was in hell?

TRENT: That's a tough one, especially if it were my child.

DAVID: It would be like trying to be happy at Christmas dinner knowing that a maniac was torturing your daughter in some secluded cabin in the woods.

TRENT: Remember what I said about analogies? In your example, the pain comes from knowing my daughter is the victim of a heinous crime. But imagine if my daughter were the serial killer, and I tried to have Christmas dinner knowing she's in prison for her crimes. I probably would be sad thinking about what she's become, but I would know that what's happening to her is just. I wouldn't be broken in the same way I would if she were an innocent victim of a madman's cruelty.

DAVID: I feel like there's always some madman or psycho waiting in the wings of our thought experiments.

TRENT: Yeah, you and I need to start watching more

> The damned may be separated from God in a relational rather than a metaphysical sense.

Hallmark Channel and less *Dateline*. In any case, if we see the damned in hell as receiving just punishments, we then see things the way God does, and we won't be sad, because we will love God more than anything, anyone, or any sin.

If loved ones are damned, we will perfectly understand God's justice toward them and his mercy toward us.

DAVID: Come on, Trent. Take away the abstractions and imagine it's *your* son with his cute cheeks and blonde curly hair rotting away in hell.

TRENT: My son is baptized and under the age of reason, or when he's accountable for personal sins . . .

Could you still believe in hell even if it means being open to the possibility of your child being damned?

DAVID: Fine, imagine him a few years older. What parent could spout the antiseptic explanation you just gave me while watching his child perish?

TRENT: I don't know how I could bear the sight of my son having such a permanent and terrifying fate. But I do know that it would be the ultimate test: "He who loves son or daughter more than me is not worthy of me" (Matt. 10:37).

DAVID: So whom are you going to pick?

TRENT: The God who gave me the gift of my children in the first place. I won't make the mistake that the mother in C.S. Lewis's *Great Divorce* makes in choosing to be in hell with her son instead of being with God in heaven. This line sticks out to me: "I don't believe in a God who keeps mother and son apart. I believe in a God of love. No one has a right to come between me and my son. Not even God. Tell him that to his face. I want my boy, and I mean to have him. He is mine, do you understand? Mine, mine, mine, for ever and ever."[9]

But my children aren't mine. My life isn't even mine. It's all a gift from God, and I have no right to demand anything from him.

Why would God make someone he knows will go to hell?

DAVID: It kind of disturbs me that you have something as horrible as hell so neatly and logically laid out in your mind.

TRENT: It's well thought out *because* hell disturbs me. My mind has been forced to think about it and come to these conclusions. But there are still tough issues I haven't fully resolved.

DAVID: I bet. For example, why would God make someone he knows will go to hell?

TRENT: I don't know. There are a few reasons that come to my mind but none that fully answers the question. First, it may be better for that person to have existence at all, even if he's damned, than to have nonexistence.

DAVID: But Jesus said of Judas that it would be better for him never to have been born (Matt. 26:24).

TRENT: Jesus said a lot of things we shouldn't take literally, like that you should cut off your hand or gouge out your eye (Matt. 5:30). In those cases, Jesus is saying it's better to give up something familiar that you love than to perish holding on to it in hell. But I can see how it would be hard to accept that hellish existence is better than nonexistence, even if the punishment glorifies God's justice and contains some kind of goodness in its own right.

Another reason I'm partial to is that if God didn't make some damned people, then those people would have veto power over their saved descendants and keep them out of heaven.

Maybe some people are permitted to be damned so that their lives will contribute to others being saved.

DAVID: What do you mean?

TRENT: Well, imagine Bob is an awful person who will be damned. However, his three children all become saints. Maybe they do so because they don't want to be miserable like their father. If God didn't create Bob to spare him from hell, then Bob's children would never enjoy heaven. As I said, why should Bob's bad decisions preclude other people being able to spend eternity with God?

DAVID: But it sounds as though you're saying some people exist only so that others can go to heaven. That sounds as if God uses people as means instead of as ends in themselves. Moreover, why couldn't God just create Bob's children in other circumstances apart from Bob?

TRENT: I don't think those people are being used because God is just respecting their free choices. Also, I'm skeptical about whether it is possible to make "Bob's children" without making them children of Bob. God could make people who are a lot like these individuals, but I don't see how they would be the *same* people.

But I do admit these are just ideas about how to resolve the problem, not full-fledged defenses.

DAVID: So you've got nothing else for me?

TRENT: Well, there is another proposal that says God doesn't know that a person will freely choose to go to hell until *after* the person is created. God knows only what a person will do in the actual world, not what we would do in any hypothetical ones he might create.

Counterfactual Knowledge

A counterfactual is a claim about something that could have happened in different circumstances. It includes claims like "if you had invited me, I would have gone to the party" or "if I had been born in the year 2500 B.C., I would not have been a Christian." There is a debate among philosophers over whether counterfactual statements are true since they don't describe events that actually happened. Since God knows only true things, those who say counterfactuals aren't true claim that God doesn't know them. Therefore, it may be the case that God doesn't know if someone will choose to go to hell until after the person is created.

DAVID: Ah, it's not God's fault. He didn't know!

TRENT: The defender of this view would say God's omnipotence allows him always to bring about good, no matter what we choose. But we have to be careful when we use words like *after*, such as "after God creates the world." God is timeless, so he wasn't ignorant in one moment of time and then learned about our damnation in the moment he created the universe. We would just say this knowledge comes *logically* after his knowledge of the created, actual world.

DAVID: You're going to have to try again, because a lot of that went over my head.

TRENT: To be honest, I'm not persuaded by this

approach to the problem, but I'll do my best to explain it, because some people do find the approach helpful. Basically, when God chooses to make a certain world, he can't know what we will freely do in that world until the world exists. Prior to that point, there are only possibilities, and God knows all of those. Once the world is created, God, through his omnipotence, can now take his complete knowledge of what we will do and arrange the universe so that his will is always done.

DAVID: But you aren't convinced . . .

TRENT: Well, I just have a hard time seeing how God can create a world if he's ignorant of what will happen in such a possible world. Plus I think counterfactuals are true, so God must know them. In fact, there is one counterfactual that really bothers me about hell.

DAVID: Really? What's that?

TRENT: Imagine a child born to a loving, Catholic family, but he ends up kidnapped. He then gets raised in a horrifically abusive situation and turns into a monstrous adult who freely rejects God. After he dies, his rebellious soul is damned to hell for all eternity. It's hard to shake the feeling that if a simple event in this child's life had been different, if he just hadn't been left at the bus stop one fall morning, then he would never have ended up in hell. To me it seems maddeningly unfair, and I don't understand why God would allow this.

DAVID: And you're confident that if this child had not been kidnapped and been raised by his family, he would be saved?

> "We know that in everything God works for good with those who love him, who are called according to his purpose" (Rom. 8:28).

TRENT: I admit it is possible that this child could still be damned. I know people raised in amazing Catholic families who still become atheists. But I also think it's plausible that this child would not have started down such a dark path were it not for such a dark event in his life. He shouldn't be punished for something outside his control that hijacked his entire way of seeing the world.

DAVID: Well, don't look to me for answers. I'm the voice of doubt!

TRENT: The only consolation I have is that God would not allow someone to be damned if the only reason they reject him was because of factors beyond his control. I mean, there are many people who grow up in awful circumstances, and they persevere to become saints. And there are people given every luxury in life who become depraved monsters. If God is good, I trust that anyone in hell is there because of his free choices and not because the weight of suffering broke his spirits. At least that's what I hope, and sometimes all you can do is hope and pray.

Can we control our rejection of God if the circumstances that shape us are outside our control?

CHAPTER 6

The Problem with Proofs for God

DAVID: So far, the answer to your doubts hinges on there being a perfectly good God who will right every wrong and make everything well. He can do that even when some people are damned for all eternity.

TRENT: More or less.

DAVID: But suppose this God didn't exist?

TRENT: We're going to be here for a while if you want to debate the existence of God.

DAVID: No need for that. I have just a few objections for you to consider. For example, what about the argument from consensus *against* the existence of God?

TRENT: I'm familiar with this kind of argument *for* God. Basically, lots of people believe in God, so how could they be wrong? It's a pretty weak argument, so I'm not sure how an atheistic version is going to help you.

DAVID: Hear me out. People are, by now, pretty good at solving mysteries and figuring things out. If there really were a God, then we'd expect the brightest people among us to gradually gather around that idea and form a consensus. But they don't. In fact, ninety-three percent of the members of the National Academy of Scientists are atheists.[10]

If God exists, why don't the experts all agree that he exists?

Appeal to Authority

We believe things we're told because we trust the authorities (teachers, textbooks, etc.) who tell us. However, some authorities may be trustworthy on some topics, but not others. Being smart in one field of study does not mean a person will be equally informed in every other subject. Trent is saying it is a fallacy, or an error of reasoning, to say scientists are experts on the existence of God just because there is one field of study (a particular branch of science) where they do excel.

TRENT: Okay, that statement has a *ton* of assumptions packed into it.

DAVID: No, it doesn't. I bet it kills you that the smartest people in the world don't believe in God.

TRENT: Who says these are the "smartest people" in the world? There is no test that tells us an atheistic physicist is "smarter" than a Christian with a Ph.D. in a non-scientific field like mathematics or ancient history. Plus, I've heard some of these scientists botch areas outside their area of expertise, like when astrophysicist Neil deGrasse Tyson claimed that all penguins live in the southern hemisphere even though Galapagos penguins live north of the equator. They may know a lot about their particular branches of science, but that doesn't mean they know a lot about the reasons for and against believing in God.

Who says celebrity scientists are the experts on everything?

Celebrity scientists are at least really smart, so why don't they believe?

Outspoken atheists are a small minority of scientists.

DAVID: These scientists aren't perfect, but they are really good at reasoning. If they aren't impressed by arguments for the existence of God, then why should you be?

TRENT: I'd like to do that unpacking of your assumptions now. The National Academy of Scientists makes up only about one percent of all scientists. That would be like judging geniuses as a whole based on the views of people in MENSA (the society for people with high IQs). Most smart people have no interest in joining a club dedicated to celebrating how smart they are, so it's not a good way to determine what most smart people believe. I know of a 2009 study that says about half of scientists believe in God or some kind of higher power.[11] True, there's a lot more non-belief among scientists than the general public, but it may be the case that non-belief leads to science instead of the other way around.

DAVID: What do you mean?

TRENT: A lot of people say they became atheists in high school and college. If that's true of these scientists, then your statistic only proves that atheists like to become scientists, not that scientists like to become atheists.[12] Besides, the biggest issue I have is that the question of God's existence is outside the expertise of most scientists. Biologists and physicists have the same advantage as mechanics and accountants when it comes to answering the question "does God exist?"

DAVID: Give me a break! A biologist is more than qualified to say the argument that our cells are proof we were "intelligently designed" is bogus. Physicists are the people we should look to, not Christian apologists, when it comes to questions about the ultimate cause of the universe.

Who are the real experts on the existence of God?

TRENT: I agree that there are empirical facts in the arguments for God's existence that some scientists are in a good position to discuss. For example, if your argument is basically "evolution is false; therefore, God exists," then an evolutionary biologist would be best qualified to attack that argument's main premise. But the best arguments for God's existence rely on truths that can be known from reason rather than scientific investigation.

Scientists can be experts regarding scientific facts in theistic arguments, but they aren't experts in the discipline of making arguments.

DAVID: So you're saying God's existence is a philosophical question and therefore we should look to philosophers to see if he exists?

TRENT: I'm saying they are probably the best equipped to answer the question.

DAVID: Well, if that's the case, then you're still in trouble: the majority of professional philosophers are atheists.[13]

TRENT: You can't answer philosophical questions by doing a head count. You need to examine the arguments for a position, and most philosophers haven't done the necessary study to address the question of God's existence.

DAVID: Come on! Every time I show you that the experts don't believe in God, you just say, "Well, those experts aren't qualified. They haven't done their homework." Face it: the only people qualified to answer the question of God's existence are the minority of philosophers who say God exists, right?

TRENT: Can I explain?

DAVID: All right . . . go ahead.

If God's existence is a philosophical issue, what does it mean that the majority of philosophers are atheists?

Are the only qualified experts philosophers who believe in God?

Scientism

Scientism is the view that the only beliefs we can be certain of, or at least *most* certain of, are scientific beliefs. But scientism is self-refuting. There is no scientific way to prove that the only knowledge we can trust is scientific. Moreover, even if scientific conclusions are reliable, there are many questions about morality and human experience that fall outside the powers of science to answer, but where philosophy can be a great help.

TRENT: *Philosophy* is a broad discipline. Philosophers who have spent most of their careers studying ethics, for example, usually haven't done the necessary reading to speak authoritatively on other issues like the nature of consciousness. When it comes to God, I've read philosophers, even chairs of departments at major universities, who have published some of the most amateur arguments for atheism. Stuff like "if God exists, can he make a rock too heavy for him to lift?"[14] To call their arguments *sophomoric* would be an insult to the sophomores they teach![15]

DAVID: Let's get real for a minute. What I'm saying is that when the evidence points to a single conclusion, experts usually gather around that conclusion. It might take some time, but eventually we get a consensus on big questions like "does the sun go around the earth?" When a position can't get a similar consensus, especially among thoughtful scientists and philosophers, then it's probably wrong.

TRENT: I'd be careful of placing that much faith in consensus.

DAVID: O ye of little faith . . .

TRENT: At one time in scientific history, it was the "consensus" that gentlemen didn't need to wash their hands in order to prevent the spread of disease, or that it was impossible that COVID-19 could have come from a laboratory. Consensus isn't all it's cracked up to be.

DAVID: Perhaps, but science also has a built-in corrective mechanism to move a consensus in favor of error into a consensus favoring truth.

TRENT: But how do you know if you live in age where the consensus is getting it right or wrong?

DAVID: You can't absolutely know, but I think peer review and other elements of science are at least reliable guides.

TRENT: Maybe to some scientific questions, but not others. Plus, philosophical questions can't be settled with experiments, so you can't form a consensus. According to a 2020 global survey, philosophers are evenly divided over fundamental issues like "which ethical theory is correct?" and "do abstract objects like numbers exist?"[16]

Philosophers who haven't studied the arguments for God are as qualified as scientists or laypeople who have done the same amount of study.

Do philos-
ophers cut
quirky, non-
religious
positions a
break?

In addition, because we're talking about God, I think a lot of philosophers (like a lot of people) don't approach the issue fairly.

DAVID: What evidence do you have for that accusation?

TRENT: When philosophers talk about unusual *non-re-ligious* positions, a lot of them don't accept those positions, but they won't have outright contempt for them, either. Consider a view like *modal realism*. This is the belief that, basically, an infinite number of other universes (or *possible worlds*) exists.[17] When we say something is *possible*, we mean that it has real existence—but in some other world besides our own. For example, when we say, "I could have been an atheist," under modal realism, we would be talking about a world that exists but isn't part of our reality—a world in which I in fact *am* an atheist.

DAVID: It's kind of fun to think there's a version of us writing the opposite of this book, where an atheist confronts his doubts about atheism.

TRENT: And that's possible! I'm open to things like the multiverse existing, but saying every possible world exists is an even grander claim than that. Many of the philosophers who reject modal realism talk about how interesting it is and even leave the door open to rehabilitate the arguments in defense of it. The same thing happens in ethics with radical proposals like anti-natalism, or the idea that it's always wrong to bring people into existence. Many philosophers disagree with this idea, but they still have a respect for the view and see room for it to grow in the face of criticism.

DAVID: But they don't do the same with religious minority views?

TRENT: Some are fair, but many other philosophers have this really dismissive tone and say things like, "All the arguments for the existence of God were refuted centuries ago."[18] To which I say, "Really? All of them? No new ones have been developed in the centuries since? And if they have, are they totally without merit?"

The death of arguments for the existence of God has been greatly exaggerated.

DAVID: Well . . . yes. Or at least they all have a weak link I'd like to talk about.

CHAPTER 7

Do Proofs Get You a Personal God?

TRENT: So what's your remaining problem with the proofs for God's existence?

DAVID: They don't get you all the way to God—that's the problem. They might get you to an *uncaused cause*, but once you get there, Christian philosophers shoehorn in God's attributes by saying, "And of course this cause is all-knowing and all-good." Like when Aquinas lazily says in the discussion of the Five Ways, "And by this everyone means God." How do they know that? Why couldn't the uncaused cause be an unconscious force or an imperfect deity?

TRENT: First, Aquinas was just giving helpful summaries of theology, not a robust refutation of atheism, so cut him a little slack. Second, arguments for God should be evaluated on what they try to prove, not on whether they prove that God exists.

DAVID: Arguments for God? Don't have to prove God exists. Okay . . .

TRENT: For example, if the contingency argument shows that a being exists that simply *must exist* by nature, we're not going to tolerate just leaving that huge revelation to sit on the table. We'd rightfully ask, "What *is* this necessary being?"

DAVID: It could be a necessary force or some other foundational reality. Why think it is a person? The cosmological arguments for God give you a cause of the universe, but they can't show that this cause is a person like you or me.

TRENT: What do you mean by *person*?

> ### Person
> An individual substance with a rational nature. A *person* is a kind of being ordered toward rationality. David says Trent might be able to prove there is an uncaused cause, but not that this cause is a person we ought to worship.

DAVID: A *someone*. A conscious entity that knows it exists and that you and I exist. When it comes to God, this would be a being that knows everything. The problem with these proofs is that they tell us only what God *is not* instead of what God is. God is not material, not

Is the real problem that arguments for God prove only that a vague cause exists, not a being with divine attributes?

Why can't the ultimate cause be a mindless force?

temporal, not contingent, not evil, not limited, etc. What is God?

TRENT: God just is.

DAVID: Cute.

TRENT: No, I'm serious. We have to remember that God is not a *being* or *creature* like the rest of us.

DAVID: Then why can't God be a force?

TRENT: What is a force?

DAVID: You know, it's the stuff that makes stuff do . . . stuff.

TRENT: Right. I think the problem here is that you're thinking of forces as if they were invisible things that exist out there and settle upon matter. But the four fundamental forces of the universe—gravity, electromagnetism, and the strong and weak nuclear forces—are just ways of describing how objects like atoms interact with one another. If there were no objects, then there would be no forces.

DAVID: I still don't see how you can get to God having knowledge and being a person from all of this.

TRENT: For me personally, if the moral or design arguments work, then I think they definitely point to a personal cause of the universe. Only persons can be designers, and morality can't exist without persons. But the cosmological arguments can get there, too, based on what we know about the uncaused cause of the universe.

It's easier to know what God is not than what God is.

Forces are just ways of describing how physical objects interact.

DAVID: But that's what I'm trying to tell you: you know only what the cause is not. You don't know what the cause is.

TRENT: Okay, let me ask you this: the uncaused cause of the universe has to be material or immaterial, right?

DAVID: I don't know.

TRENT: Dude, it has to belong to one of these categories because they're comprehensive and mutually exclusive. The cause can't be kinda-sorta made of matter, or kinda-sorta immaterial. So it's either made of matter or not made of matter. Right?

DAVID: Fine. Sure.

> ### *The Law of the Excluded Middle*
>
> A law of logic that says that for every statement, either the statement is true or its negation is true. Trent is arguing that we know that the cause of the universe must either be *material* or *not material*, so if the cause cannot be made of matter, then it must be *not material*, or immaterial.

TRENT: And you said we know it's not made of matter, or immaterial.

DAVID: Right, because this cause created matter.

TRENT: My next question is, what immaterial things exist?

DAVID: I know where you're going: either it's an abstract object like a number, or it's a mind. But numbers can't

Some arguments show that a person is behind the physical or moral design of the universe.

The ultimate cause of reality must be made of matter or not be made of matter.

What kind of immaterial things could exist that have causal power except for a mind?

Arguments for God may not fully prove the existence of a being with every divine attribute, but they make atheism untenable.

cause anything, so the mind is the only option. But what if there is some mysterious third category we haven't discovered yet?

TRENT: I confess that I'm not a fan of arguments that try to reach a conclusion by process of elimination. But on the other hand, all the arguments for God seem to terminate in some kind of ultimate, uncaused cause. And if such a cause exists, and it's not made of matter, that makes naturalism a really awkward view and swings the door wide open for theism.

DAVID: Whoa. How'd you reach that conclusion?

TRENT: Well, what is *naturalism*?

DAVID: It's the view the natural world is all that exists.

TRENT: I'm worried that that's a bit circular, since it doesn't tell us what *nature* is. I prefer definitions like "the foundation of reality is physical." Even if non-physical things like minds and numbers exist, the ultimate foundation of reality would be physical in some way. The non-physical would depend on the physical to exist, or at least to have any causal power. So if the ultimate foundation of the world is not physical, then naturalism seems to be false.

DAVID: But it isn't good for your position that you've reasoned your way to the ultimate cause of the universe being all-knowing or all-good just because we cannot figure out any other kind of immaterial cause that exists.

TRENT: As I said before, the design and moral arguments

do point toward some kind of personal cause of the universe.

DAVID: But you don't have a single argument that neatly proves all of God's attributes. You have to rely on all these different arguments to prop up your case.

TRENT: I don't see why that's a bad thing. In courtrooms, attorneys often use multiple lines of evidence to prove their case. I also think we have to get past this idea that God is a *person* like you or me.

DAVID: What do you mean?

TRENT: Well, he's not a person like you, because you are a figment of my imagination.

DAVID: That hurts. Imaginary people have real feelings, you know.

TRENT: "Imaginary people have real feelings" would make for a great bumper sticker. But in any case, we use the term *person* to describe the members of the Trinity, but we use the term in an analogical way. God is not a person like you, and he's not even a person like me. If God belonged to a certain kind, like how I belong to the *human* kind or *person* kind, then that kind would precede God. For example, I am now a *Texan* . . .

DAVID: Yee-haw!

TRENT: Howdy! But of course, the reference class of *Texas* existed before me. So if we say, "God is a person," that would make the category of *person* more fundamental than God. It would be something to which God

"Proofs for the existence of God" exist "in the sense of 'converging and convincing arguments,' which allow us to attain certainty about the truth" (CCC 31).

belongs. But nothing can be more fundamental than God, so it seems as though this kind of description of God is going to be untenable.

God is not a being that belongs to a kind; he is being itself and the reason why every kind of creature and thing exists.

Classical Theism

A tradition in philosophy that considers God to be radically different from all creatures because God does not belong to any class of beings. It is proper to speak of God only as *being itself* or the reason why every kind of being has existence. This stands in contrast to *theistic personalism*, which holds that God is just an unlimited example of a particular kind of being we call a *person*.

Does classical theism illicitly hide God in a veil of mystery?

DAVID: But if you say "God is being itself" or "the ground of existence," aren't you saying God is a kind of "being" or a "kind of existence," and so those things are more fundamental than God?

TRENT: No, because I've always asserted that God just *is* "being" or "existence."

DAVID: That sounds like word salad. Describe in detail what it means for God to be *being*.

TRENT: I can't.

DAVID: So it seems that you're retreating into mystery.

TRENT: I'm humbly acknowledging the limits of what reason can show me. I'd expect any honest atheist to do the same—unless you think that somehow, atheists alone have evolved past intellectual limits.

DAVID: No, atheists have evolved humility just as well as theists have.

TRENT: Then let's treat atheism and Christianity as being on a par.

DAVID: Wait, what? Why should we? Atheism is just the denial of a proposition; it doesn't affirm anything.

TRENT: Well, it does affirm either that God doesn't exist or that there are at least no good reasons to believe that God exists. But all right—lets switch it up and say "naturalism vs. theism." I don't know any naturalist who would say the ultimate foundation of reality is "immaterial, timeless, necessary, unchanging, and infinite."

Naturalism

The view that only nature exists. The term is notoriously hard to define, but it usually refers to the denial of the existence of immaterial beings like angels, ghosts, and God. It can allow for the existence of some immaterial objects that do not have causal power (for example, abstract objects like numbers) and immaterial things whose existence depends on material objects (for example, minds totally dependent on brains).

DAVID: I would say that is just the weird but non-divine ultimate foundation of reality.

TRENT: "Non-divine"? Tell me: what does it mean for something to be *natural*?

DAVID: It follows predictable laws of nature.

TRENT: Careful . . . you're using the term you're trying to define within its own definition.

DAVID: Ack! I should know better. I would say naturalism

Do the attributes of the ultimate cause of reality make more sense under theism or atheism/naturalism?

Naturalism often involves a circular definition: the claim that only nature exists and that nature is just that which actually exists.

Should theists have a single argument that proves that a cause with all divine attributes exists?

holds that all of reality is either explainable through predictable interactions involving matter and energy or at least grounded in those things. Our minds, for example, might be immaterial entities not bound by physical laws, but under naturalism, their existence would ultimately dependent upon physical brains. The "basement" of reality is matter and energy.

TRENT: So if a proof for God shows that the "basement" of reality is actually the negation, or *not* matter and energy, then it seems as though naturalism is refuted.

The proofs for theism are superior to any form of naturalism that can't explain the timeless, immaterial, and unchanging cause of reality.

DAVID: Or there is some other weird "third way." You still don't have a single proof that shows there is a cause with all of the "omni-attributes" we associate with God, especially omniscience.

TRENT: Some classic proofs for God (like the *argument from motion*) do not straightforwardly reveal God's "mental attributes" like omniscience, though I think there are ways they can strongly point in that direction.[19] But this isn't an unsolvable problem because other proofs (for example, design, moral arguments) do point toward the cause being personal and complement proofs that show that the cause is without limits (for example, argument from motion, contingency arguments). Also, the proofs themselves cut against core commitments of naturalism like foundational materialism. Finally, there is evidence that this God is an "unlimited person," if I can use that term carefully, based on what God has revealed to mankind.

DAVID: Well, let's talk about that, then, since even if there is an *uncaused cause* out there, you don't have much of a religion if it can be shown that this cause hasn't revealed itself to humanity.

CHAPTER 8

Anything but a Resurrection

Do apologists have too many convenient explanations for Bible difficulties?

DAVID: You know what? I was going to grill you on all sorts of embarrassing things in the Old Testament. We could have spent hours just talking about the parts of the Bible where God orders the Israelites to slaughter men, women, and children.

TRENT: And I would have shared a variety of ways a person could approach those difficulties. We could talk about God's authority to give and take life because he is the author of life or the possibility that these texts don't literally describe . . .

DAVID: It's not literal! It's not literal! Do you literally believe in anything the Bible says?

TRENT: I believe that Jesus' glorified flesh and blood are literally received through bread and wine.

DAVID: That's cute, but I'm going to hop over all the

Bible difficulties and go to the biggest one: the Resurrection.

TRENT: Why's that?

DAVID: You have some good replies to these Bible difficulties, but you have to admit there are passages in Scripture that are difficult to understand.

TRENT: Yes, there are parts of the Old Testament that make me wince or feel embarrassed, but that's not enough to say it is false because . . .

DAVID: Because! Because! Jesus of Nazareth believed in the Old Testament, and . . .

TRENT: . . . if a man can walk out of his own tomb, I'm going to trust what he trusted, and Jesus believed that the Old Testament is the word of God.

DAVID: That's a clever reply, but now you're pressing all of your faith on this one event. You can say, "Well, even if there isn't evidence for the Exodus . . ."

TRENT: *Specific, corroborating non-biblical evidence* for the Exodus. The biblical account is evidence for the Exodus . . .

DAVID: Whatever, or even if the Bible has those pesky parts about killing women and children, you can say, "I know there *has* to be a solution to these problems because . . . Jesus." But now you've made so much rely on the truth of the Resurrection that I don't think even Jesus could move this mountain of objections if it blocked his tomb.

> The Bible can be difficult to understand because of Scripture's remote and unfamiliar cultural and historical setting.

> Every apparent contradiction in Scripture is apparent because we know that Jesus rose from the dead, and he believed in Scripture.

TRENT: What's wrong with making the Resurrection the cornerstone of my faith? St. Paul even said, "If Christ has not been raised, your faith is futile and you are still in your sins" (1 Cor. 15:17).

Is it a good idea to make Christianity stand or fall on the truth of Jesus' resurrection?

DAVID: So you won't take the "non-literal" approach if my objections get too difficult and say the story of Easter is really a story about having a "resurrection of hope" or "faith in faith."

It makes no sense to "have faith in faith."

TRENT: Yeah, I can't stand that stuff. I'd rather be an atheist than a Christian whose God is a bunch of platitudes. I mean, what does it mean to "have faith in faith"? That's like saying, "I'm in love with love." You can love the *idea* of love in the sense of recognizing love's goodness, but I can't be in love with the abstract concept of love. Likewise, I don't "have faith in faith," or think that just being "trusting" will save me from my sins. Only trusting in Jesus Christ, who is true God and true man, can do that.

What is the weak point in defenses of the Resurrection?

DAVID: But why should anyone believe that Jesus is "true God and true man"?

TRENT: Primarily because Jesus vindicated his claims to being divine through his bodily resurrection from the dead.

DAVID: All right, I'm not going to hash out your entire apologetic on this, but I will go for its weakest point.

TRENT: I'm ready.

DAVID: You say the Resurrection best explains facts like the empty tomb, the disciples' experiences of seeing

Jesus after his death, and their radical transformation into missionaries willing to be martyrs.

TRENT: Correct.

DAVID: But why can't we just say this was a weird example of people committing fraud or having hallucinations on a mass scale?

TRENT: Because we don't have examples of people enduring martyrdom for obvious lies or an entire group of people hallucinating the same thing.

DAVID: You know what we also don't have examples of? People rising from the dead three days after they died! How can you confidently say, "These kinds of hallucinations don't happen" or "These kinds of frauds don't happen," and therefore it was a resurrection? A resurrection is the one thing we agree doesn't happen outside the cases under dispute.

TRENT: I'm not saying that what happened to Jesus was some weird hiccup in the natural order that caused Jesus to come back to life. If that were the case, then there are other weird hiccups I'd be inclined to go with before concluding that a resurrection had happened. I'm saying Jesus *miraculously* rose from the dead, and so if a person's worldview allows for miracles to occasionally occur, then that hypothesis should be put on the table with other natural explanations.

DAVID: Okay, so why not say this was a *miraculous* hallucination, and God caused the apostles to believe that Jesus rose from the dead when he actually didn't?

A natural resurrection would be as unlikely as other natural explanations, but God miraculously raising Jesus from the dead is not subject to the same unlikelihood.

TRENT: Because then you would have God, who is the standard of goodness itself, directly causing and spreading the biggest lie the world has ever known. That's a theory I would say has the same probability as a married bachelor: zero.

DAVID: Aliens.

TRENT: What?

DAVID: Advanced aliens decided to mess with humanity by stealing Jesus' body and then used hologram technology to make people think Jesus rose from the dead.

TRENT: That's a stretch, don't you think?

DAVID: We know that holograms exist, and there could be aliens in the universe. At least it's a natural explanation and not a supernatural one.

TRENT: I don't divide reality into natural and supernatural worlds that we pit against each other. Some fields, like science, don't speak to the supernatural because they study only fundamental elements of nature like matter and energy. But that doesn't mean reality consists of only matter and energy. If we have good reasons to believe God that exists, then we should be open to instances where God reveals himself to mankind.

DAVID: So why is God more likely than aliens in this case?

TRENT: I would say it's less *ad hoc.* An explanation might be able to explain everything, but if there's no reason to initially point to that explanation, then we shouldn't

Miraculous deception is so improbable that it may not even count as a possible explanation.

Are aliens more plausible than a God-man who miraculously rises from the dead?

rely on it. In college, my bike got stolen during class. Aliens transporting it explains the missing bike and lock, but there's no reason to suppose aliens did it when human bike thieves will suffice.

But the people involved in the Resurrection all attribute it to God, and they don't describe things like spaceships or advanced technology that would be better attributed to aliens. So there's some reason to posit God as the explanation for this event and no reason to posit aliens.

In this respect, we can follow a simple rule of reality: things are as they appear unless evidence suggests otherwise. All the evidence surrounding Christ's resurrection doesn't have the appearance of alien involvement, but it at least *appears* to be a miracle.

> We shouldn't rush to supernatural explanations, but neither should we prefer any unlikely natural explanation before we consider a supernatural one.

Ad Hoc

A Latin phrase that means "to this" or "this purpose." When used to describe explanations, it refers to ones that are designed to account for evidence but have no specific evidence for them. In this case, Trent is saying that mischievous aliens might explain the facts related to the Resurrection, but there is no evidence for these specific aliens (for example, descriptions of spaceships in the Gospels). However, there is evidence—which doesn't include aliens—for God's existence and his propensity to reveal himself.

DAVID: But appearances can be deceiving. There's no reason to suppose God raised Jesus from the dead when merely human hallucinations will suffice.

CHAPTER 9

Resurrecting the Hallucination Theory

Can the hallucination theory be salvaged as a natural explanation for the origin of Resurrection belief?

DAVID: All right, let's get more down to earth. Why can't the hallucination theory explain the origin of Christianity? The apostles sincerely *thought* Jesus rose from the dead, even though he actually didn't.

TRENT: Because this isn't just one person claiming to have seen Jesus in something like a dream. If that had been the case, then I could see overactive imaginations being a plausible explanation, but it wasn't. To make a comparison: when you read the only account of the first-century wonderworker Apollonius of Tyana, you see that his supposed "resurrection" was just somebody waking up from having a dream about him being alive. But the Gospels and Paul's letter to the Corinthians confirm that Jesus appeared to multiple people, including groups of people. And speaking of Paul: he had been a persecutor of the Church when Jesus appeared to him, not a follower of Christ, so he had no reason to imagine a hopeful hallucination about Jesus rising from the dead. The hallucination theory really lacks explanatory power, in my opinion.

> **Hallucination Theory**
>
> This is any theory that proposes to account for the disciples' unprecedented belief that Jesus rose from the dead. David believes that Trent has refuted only weaker versions of the hallucination theory and wants to know why it can't provide a natural explanation for the origin of Christianity.

One reason the hallucination theory is inadequate is that it can't explain Jesus' appearances to groups of disciples and enemies of the Faith, such as Paul.

DAVID: And the Resurrection doesn't? Why not just say the apostles had some weird experience we don't understand, whether you want to call it a hallucination or not? That's still more probable than a resurrection, which has never been conclusively proven ever to have happened.

Why believe in an unknown kind of resurrection over an unknown kind of hallucination?

TRENT: What kind of probability theory are you using? If it's just based on frequency, or on the number of verified resurrections that have occurred, then you could never prove that any unique event ever happened in history. Why believe that the Big Bang caused the expansion of the universe, for example, when no one has ever observed a Big Bang before?

DAVID: But can't you even entertain the possibility that this was just a case of "social contagion" or mass hysteria?

TRENT: What do you mean?

If previously unobserved and unrepeatable events are always too improbable to be an explanation, then we have to say goodbye to similar, well-accepted explanations such as the Big Bang.

DAVID: For example, here's what might have happened with the Resurrection. Peter is grief-stricken and guilty about how he denied Jesus. Then, after the Crucifixion, Peter prays asking Jesus to forgive him and then he hears Jesus' voice in his head saying, "I forgive you." He then tells the other apostles Jesus is risen, and before you know it, they all start hearing Jesus' voice and saying the same thing . . . and then the Resurrection legend has taken on a life of its own.

TRENT: But what about the Gospel accounts showing that this isn't just a "disembodied voice" that people heard? We have a Jesus who can be touched and who eats fish in the presence of his disciples (Luke 24:43).

Were the post-Resurrection appearances just apologetic legends?

DAVID: That could all be made up as part of the legend. We know that in the early Church there was a heresy called Docetism that said Jesus only *appeared* to be human. Details like Jesus eating fish could have been added to fight this particular heresy. There's no reason to think they were part of the original story, since Paul never says anything about it.

TRENT: Or . . .

DAVID: Or what?

TRENT: *Or*, this is what we'd expect if Jesus rose from the dead. I mean, imagine if people thought you were dead.

DAVID: I'm a figment of your imagination, so I'm already halfway there.

TRENT: Right. Well, if people were absolutely convinced that *I* was dead, when they saw me they would think I was a ghost. When the disciples saw Jesus walking on water, they thought he was a ghost (Mark 6:49). After an angel rescued Peter from prison, a maid named Rhoda announced Peter's presence but those in the house said she must have seen "his angel" instead (Acts 12:15). A quick way to show someone you're not a ghost, a pure spirit, would be to eat something.

Does the hallucination theory also require explanations no one's observed before?

DAVID: Or it's what the experts say it is—an apologetic legend.

Docetism

From the Greek word *dokein,* which means "to seem," this early heresy claimed that Jesus was not truly human, with a real human body, but that his body was merely a phantasm. 1 John 4:3 may be referring to these heretics when it refers to "every spirit which does not confess Jesus is not of God."

TRENT: Perhaps, but if these appearances were supposed to combat Docetism, why would they include details that Docetists might use to their advantage, like Jesus preventing people from recognizing him (Luke 24:16), disappearing from people's sight (Luke 24:31), or appearing in rooms with "shut doors" (John 20:21, 26)? Also, the social contagion theory seems to commit what you consider the same errors of the Resurrection theory.

DAVID: I find that hard to believe, since I'm appealing to things that we all know exist, like hallucinations, and

Could the post-Resurrection appearances just be mass hysteria?

you are using things we don't know exist, like God and resurrections.

TRENT: How many people do you know who think they once heard their dead grandma's voice conclude that grandma must still be alive? I'll grant you that grief-induced hallucinations do occur (though some of them might actually be contact with the deceased!), but typically the people who have those experiences still think their loved one is dead. Also, how many cases do you know of involving multiple people having the *same* grief-induced hallucination? How many cases involve one person's testimony causing another person to have the same hallucination?

DAVID: I'm not sure, but I bet there are cases like that out there.

TRENT: Sounds like your skeptical view of the Resurrection also has an element of faith built into it. In fact, a few years ago a physician named Joseph Bergeron surveyed thousands of cases in the medical literature and could not find a single case of a group grief hallucination comparable to the group appearances described in the New Testament.[20]

DAVID: I know you like to say groups don't have hallucinations, but what about *dancing hysteria* in the Middle Ages, where entire villages engaged in crazy bouts of dancing? Or cult members who all say they saw the same "miracle," like the members of the murderous Manson family who say they saw their leader, Charles Manson, levitate a bus over a creek?

TRENT: Dancing hysteria cases are fascinating, but they aren't like communal resurrection appearances. These people are all *acting* the same way, but they aren't all reporting to have *seen* the same thing that doesn't exist.

DAVID: Okay, but what about the Manson family?

TRENT: Contrary to what some skeptics insinuate,[21] it was actually just one guy, eighteen-year-old Clem Grogan, who claimed he saw Manson do this. And the judge at his trial said, "Grogan was too stupid and too hopped on drugs to decide anything on his own."[22] Frankly, I'm surprised he didn't see weirder things while using LSD. As for "dancing hysteria," it could have been caused by hallucinogenic fungal molds or even just by people just trying to "dance off" the drudgery of medieval life. Have you ever seen the *Candid Camera* episode where everyone faces the rear of an elevator when the doors open?

> Mass hysteria usually involves the spread of strange behaviors (e.g. dancing, laughing), not unprecedented beliefs.

Mass Hysteria

Occurs when collective illusions, usually of threats, spread through a population via fear and rumors. David believes that accounts of Jesus rising from the dead being mass hysteria are a plausible natural explanation for the origin of Resurrection belief.

DAVID: Sure, most people who get into an elevator end up following the crowd and looking to the back of the elevator out of peer pressure.

TRENT: I think that's what was happening in a lot of

Does St. Paul's conversion have a natural explanation?

these "mass hysteria" cases. But, in the ancient world, the prevailing peer pressure would have been to believe that Jesus was a failed messiah or that God had taken Jesus' soul up to heaven, not that Jesus rose in a glorified body. Also, hallucinations wouldn't explain why someone like St. Paul converted. He had no reason to have a grief-induced hallucination about Jesus, given that he relentlessly persecuted the Church until his conversion.

DAVID: All right, how about this? Paul had an epileptic episode, which caused him to go blind, and after a Christian prayed over him, he came to believe that it was Jesus who helped him "see." His being an epileptic and the residual damage to his vision would explain the "thorn in the flesh" he complained about (2 Cor. 12:6-7), why he wrote in large letters (Gal. 6:11), and why some people wanted to give him their own eyes (Gal. 4:15).

TRENT: Intriguing theory, but I'm not convinced.

DAVID: Of course you aren't.

TRENT: Epileptic blindness is common in children, not adults, and when it does happen to adults, they don't know they are blind because of miscommunication in the brain.[23] This kind of blindness also goes away gradually, so this doesn't match the description of Paul's conversion in Acts (not to mention that Paul's companions were also partially aware of the experience). But more importantly, if Paul routinely suffered from epileptic fits, then we'd expect his opponents to accuse him of being demonically possessed . . .

DAVID: Well, maybe they did . . .

TRENT: . . . and if they did, we'd expect to find Paul's defense against that accusation in his letters, just as we read his defense of his character against other charges—for example, that he is persuasive only by letter and not in person (2 Cor. 10:10) or that he lacked the credentials to be an apostle (11:5-6).

    Honestly, the Resurrection just has so much more going for it than other cases involving mental illness or mass hysteria. It has the conversion of non-disciples, a tomb nearby where you could verify if the body was still there, persecution to root out fraud . . .

DAVID: Yeah, but you're not being consistent. If you applied those same standards to other religions, you'd have to believe in them, too.

The absence of charges that Paul was demonically possessed counts against the claim that epileptic seizures caused Paul's conversion.

Mass hysteria still doesn't explain things like the empty tomb.

CHAPTER 10

A Miraculous Double Standard?

TRENT: Like what?

Could arguments for the Resurrection also prove Mormonism is true?

DAVID: Didn't Joseph Smith, the founder of Mormonism, show he sincerely believed in the Book of Mormon by being willing to die for it? And the Book of Mormon includes the testimony of eight witnesses who saw Smith's "golden plates" that allegedly came from an angel. Three of them all saw an angel show them the plates at the same time. And since group hallucinations are impossible, this means Mormonism must be true!

TRENT: Wow, that's a lot of false equivalencies packed into one counterexample, but let's draw out one thread at a time. First, the idea that Joseph Smith was "willing to die" for the Book of Mormon. I'm calling shenanigans on that.

DAVID: You don't even know what that means.

TRENT: I know it has something to do with pointing out false or misleading claims, even if I don't have the term's whole backstory. When it comes to Smith, I agree that portraying himself as a prophet entailed a lot of risk.

How do we know the apostles *chose* to die for the Gospel?

DAVID: Then he must have really believed he was a prophet.

TRENT: Or, like many charlatans, he was willing to tolerate a lot of risk for what he considered to be a lot of rewards. During his life he acquired a significant following and even became the mayor of a city. He also procured dozens of "spiritual wives" for himself, some as young as fourteen years old.[24]

DAVID: Funny how all these self-acclaimed male prophets usually end up saying that God wants them to have lots of wives.

TRENT: Except we don't find anything like that in the New Testament. Instead, the apostles left everything in their lives behind to follow Jesus (Matt 19:27). The only reward waiting for them were painful persecution at the hands of groups like the Sanhedrin and Roman officials. Smith eventually died in a shootout in a county jail— unlike Peter, Paul, and the other apostles who peacefully submitted to unjust executions so that their deaths would be a witness of their sincere faith.

DAVID: But how do you know the apostles weren't "charlatans" like Smith? Maybe the Romans just chopped off their heads or put them on crosses before they had a chance to admit it.

TRENT: I don't think that's likely, given that we have a letter from a Roman emperor at the beginning of the second century, Trajan, who gives instructions on what to do with people accused of being Christian. He said, "They are not to be sought out; if they are denounced and proved guilty, they are to be punished, with this reservation, that whoever denies that he is a Christian and really proves it—that is, by worshiping our gods—even though he was under suspicion in the past, shall obtain pardon through repentance."[25]

That sounds like the apostles certainly could have backed out, if in fact they were phonies and their preaching was now getting out of hand.

DAVID: But you don't have any source specifically describing the apostles refusing to recant and accepting martyrdom, do you?

TRENT: We don't have anything that specific. But 1 Clement 5, written in the first century, says that Peter and Paul were martyred, and Josephus says that James, the "brother of the Lord," was stoned for breaking the Law.

DAVID: But we don't know if their deaths had anything to do with their preaching of the Resurrection. So can you even say with confidence that these apostles died for Jesus?

TRENT: What I can confidently say is that the apostles were willing to endure suffering and even death for preaching that Jesus was the Messiah. Even if you dispute the evidence for the martyrdom of the apostles, it seems clear that they did risk a lot given what is described in the book of Acts. Paul describes how he was beaten with rods, stoned, shipwrecked, and constantly in danger because of his preaching mission (2 Cor. 11:25).

We at least know for certain that the disciples were willing to risk a lot for comparatively little earthly reward.

DAVID: Even if Smith was a fraud, the other Mormon witnesses seemed to be totally sincere. What about the ones who saw an angel show them the golden plates?

TRENT: What's weird about this incident is that Smith had the plates in his possession because he was allegedly translating them, but he refused to show them to the men. Instead, Smith brought them to a wooded area and told them to pray to see the golden plates, which took some time. This could have primed the men to imagine a vision of an angel. And their claim to have seen the plates is highly qualified. Mormon author Marvin Hill says that "the three witnesses saw the plates in vision only," and one of the witnesses, Martin Harris, later said, "I did not see them as I do that pencil-case, yet I saw them with the eye of faith." Finally, these men abandoned the Mormon faith.[26] This stands in contrast to the Resurrection, since there is no report of the disciples ever abandoning the Church.

DAVID: But here's the double standard I see: when it comes to the miracles of other religions, you are the "super-skeptic" who's eager to put forward natural explanations. But when it's *your* religion, you wave away natural explanations.

TRENT: There are two problems with your assertion. First, there are many miracle accounts in my own religious tradition that I don't accept. I think some of the stories of saints performing miraculous deeds were written so long after the saint lived that they are impossible to sift from pious legends that cropped up in the same period. Second, there are miracle accounts in other traditions I'm open to accepting. These phenomena could be the work of demons or even genuine miracles.

DAVID: But why would God try to make another religion look true?

TRENT: Who's to say that's what he's doing? The true God might miraculously heal a pagan praying to a false god because he loves this person in spite of his ignorance. The person might then mistakenly attribute that healing to his religion's deity. In fact, this argument is worse for your position than mine.

DAVID: How so?

TRENT: If naturalism is true, then all of these miracle claims, near-death experiences, and similar supernatural claims must be false. And I agree that a lot of them *are* false, but if even one of them is true, then that's the end of naturalism. So what's more likely? That at least one of them is true, or all of them are false?

DAVID: What's more likely: that every account of an alien abduction is false or at least one of them is true?

TRENT: I'm not asserting that alien abduction stories are all false or that aliens don't exist. And I'm not prepared to rule them out. I'm fifty-fifty on the issue.

Some Catholic miracle claims are false, and some non-Christian miracle claims may be true.

What's more likely? That there have never been any miracles or that at least one has occurred?

DAVID: So you're going to save the Resurrection by believing in aliens?

TRENT: I'm going to humbly admit that the world is a weird place we don't fully understand. I wish all skeptics would have this attitude instead of just immediately comparing Christianity to Batman or Harry Potter or something else we definitely know is fictional.

DAVID: I personally would very much like it if Batman were real, but we don't always get what we want.

TRENT: Very true. But I get being concerned about the evidence for the Resurrection. If that amount of evidence convinces me that Jesus rose from the dead, then similar evidence should convince me of other miracle accounts. But it's interesting that when I scour the literature for other miracles with similar amounts of evidence, not many are offered outside a Christian context. In fact, the best example many atheists come up with as an alternative to the Resurrection is apparitions of the Virgin Mary.

DAVID: Yes, it's amusing to watch Protestant apologists try to wriggle out of accepting the Resurrection while also denying Marian apparitions.

TRENT: Some do, but others are quite honest about it. Mike Licona is one of the best defenders of the Resurrection today, and when it comes to Marian apparitions, he says, "Because I am Protestant, I carry a theological bias against an appearance of Mary. However, I am not predisposed to reject the reality of apparitions in general. . . . The apparitions of Mary are not necessarily natural, psychological events in the minds of the seers."[27]

If the sheer number of miracle claims makes them more likely, do we have to accept every paranormal claim?

In our mysterious world, there could be many strange things beyond resurrections that we have not confirmed yet.

DAVID: All right, last question. What would it take to convince you that Christ didn't rise from the dead? It's convenient when apologists say, "Oh, produce Jesus' body"—they know that nobody can do that, since we don't have Jesus' DNA in order to confirm that the bones we find really belonged to him.

TRENT: I agree that that's a tough bar to get over, but it doesn't have to be *that* high. Personally, if we discovered a letter saying that the apostles recanted their belief in the Resurrection—an authentic letter either written by them or by witnesses—that would cause me at least to have some significant doubts.

DAVID: But isn't it uncomfortable that your salvation, your entire life, hinges on what some 2,000-year-old documents say? That seems to be a really fragile thing upon which to balance your life.

TRENT: Evidence is like money. I wouldn't mind having more of it, but as long as I have enough to get by, then I'm okay with that. And I'm confident that's what we have when it comes to Christianity. We have enough evidence. The question is, how will we live our lives in the face of that evidence?

The same kinds of evidence for the Resurrection appearances of Jesus can be found in Marian apparitions.

What would it take to convince you Christ didn't rise from the dead?

More evidence for the Resurrection would be preferable, but the amount we do have is sufficient to justify belief.

CHAPTER 11

The Apologist vs. the Theologians

DAVID: I have a joke for you.

TRENT: Okay . . .

DAVID: Who are the best apologists for Protestantism?

TRENT: I give up.

DAVID: Catholic theologians!

TRENT: Har har . . .

DAVID: No, I'm serious. I think one of your problems is that you are trying to sell people a fantasy version of Catholicism that doesn't match the real thing.

TRENT: I thought we already got over your whole "I'm just a used-car salesman" schtick.

DAVID: No, here's what I mean. Apologists always make it sound like there's this mountain of evidence for

Catholicism. "Two thousand years of unbroken tradition," they say. But when you go to the theologians, the real experts, they tell a very different story. They admit that a lot of the Bible doesn't support Catholic doctrine and that what Catholics believe has been missing from a lot of Church history.

Do apologists present a "tidier" faith than what comes from theologians?

TRENT: And what would that be?

DAVID: Here's one. You like to argue that 1 Corinthians 3:15 proves the doctrine of purgatory because it says, "If any man's work is burned up, he will suffer loss, though he himself will be saved, but only as through fire." But the Catholic Jerusalem Bible says that "purgatory is not directly envisaged here" and the Catholic New American Bible says that this text "has sometimes been used to support the notion of purgatory, though it does not envisage this."

Theologians practice exegesis; apologists prooftext.

TRENT: Hmmm, I feel like there are two kinds of theologians you may be talking about. Some are one step away from being atheists and only say they're Catholic because of a flimsy "I have faith in faith" theology. They may be behind the absolutely dreadful footnotes in some Catholic Bibles.

DAVID: Ah, so it's not Catholicism that's to blame, it's the secret atheists who have infiltrated the Church!

TRENT: Just because someone has academic abbreviations after his name doesn't mean he's infallible. And it's oversimplistic to contrast the "theologians" who are all gung-ho for liberal theology with the super-conservative "apologists." In reality, there are lots of academic theologians who have theologically conservative views and there are popular proponents of Catholicism who are quite liberal on certain theological and moral issues. But there's a second group of theologians who'd write stuff like this that I actually don't mind too much.

There is no such thing as "theologians" and "apologists" who all believe the same thing and adopt the same methodology.

DAVID: Why's that?

TRENT: How should I put this? Sometimes when people argue for a position, they treat every piece of evidence as really strong and equally conclusive. They feel like they have mountains of evidence to share with people and they aren't particularly worried by objections. I call these people "maximalists" because they try to share the maximum amount of evidence. In contrast, a "minimalist" only relies on what he thinks is the strongest evidence for a claim. He'd rather have one argument that can't be refuted than ten arguments of varying quality, some of which aren't that hard to attack. For example, those theologians who say that Paul is not thinking of purgatory probably note that Paul is speaking about how "each man's work will become manifest; for the Day will disclose it" (1 Cor. 3:13). The "Day" is Judgment Day and Paul is talking about a final testing of works and "salvation by fire" that will take place at the final judgment.

DAVID: But the Church teaches that, for saved people who are still imperfectly purified, "after death they undergo purification" (CCC 1030). So that means Paul disagrees with the Catholic doctrine that after some sinners die they go to purgatory.

TRENT: At this point in his life, Paul probably thought the end of the world was imminent and so he conflated the end of the world with the end of our lives. But eventually Paul saw this was not the case; and so 1 Corinthians 3 shows how the verdict we receive at the particular judgment after death is reaffirmed at the final judgment at the end of the world. This shows that although a *developed* concept of purgatory may not be present in this verse, the essential feature of suffering loss because of sin and being saved through some kind of ordeal is present.

Some theologians are not as bold as apologists because they are extra cautious about the strength of their arguments.

DAVID: It sounds more like the apologist wants to hide all the difficulties associated with the Faith in some kind of theological closet while the theologian is willing to investigate "how the sausage is made."

TRENT: Once again you're generalizing (and mixing your metaphors). You're right that some apologists make extremely broad claims like, "Every Church Father taught doctrine X," which may be very hard to prove or may even be false. But that wouldn't disprove the apostolic origin of doctrine X. And I know other apologists who are much more measured in what they claim and try very hard to not overstate their case. Another problem is that, in the body of Christ, the role of theologians and apologists is different. Theologians are like the *scientists* who are out studying the data and synthesizing our knowledge. Apologists are like the *science educators* who make the science understandable for others. To continue the analogy: are you familiar with modern proponents of the flat Earth?

DAVID: They are hilarious! My favorite claim of theirs is that because the Earth is a flat disk, Antarctica is actually a huge ice wall no one has ever crossed, because the South Pole doesn't exist.

TRENT: Yes, they are . . . something . . . but there are lots of astronomers and geologists who obviously know the Earth is spherical, and can prove it, but aren't great at communicating that to people in an engaging way. Or they let themselves get verbally trampled by a flat-earther who's just really good at debating. Some of the most effective critics of flat-Earth theory are YouTubers who may be science educators rather than professional scientists. In fact, many of the people who respond to pseudo-science might make simpler claims to help people understand them that a scientist might feel the need to endlessly qualify.

> Theologians are like scientists who expand our knowledge, whereas apologists take what theologians have learned and help others learn, apply, and defend it.

DAVID: But what about Catholic historians who say that the dogma of the Assumption was "unknown" in the early Church or that there was no bishop of Rome in the first century? This doesn't seem like a case of "over-qualifying" the evidence. These Catholic scholars are saying there is no evidence for these fundamental dogmas!

TRENT: And if it isn't just a matter of nuancing a belief, then I might disagree with their arguments. Some of these theologians just make bad arguments, such as faulty "arguments from silence" that try to prove "doctrine X did not exist" because there is no explicit mention of doctrine X in some part of Church history. If I come across an objection to the Faith, it's not like my reply is going to suddenly become worthless because I discovered to my horror that the objection came from a fellow Catholic. With some theologically dubious friends in the Church, who needs enemies?!

DAVID: But doesn't it seem like apologists have this unique burden to convince other people and so they, consciously or unconsciously, twist the evidence? Whereas theologians are just free to publish on whatever topic they like and so they can be more honest about their opinions.

TRENT: Well, I know a lot of theologians who try very hard to "convince other people," so I fail to see the force of this objection. In fact, I think I can perform some apologetics judo on your argument.

DAVID: Please. You went to one Brazilian jiu-jitsu class and a black belt threw you into the mat so hard you threw up.

TRENT: One day I'll take my skills at making arguments "submit" and apply them to people, but for now I can't resist turning your argument into a pretzel. Your point seemed to be that Catholic apologists don't have credibility because sometimes they contradict or at least don't share the opinions of Catholic theologians.

DAVID: Correct.

TRENT: But by that reasoning, Protestant apologists wouldn't have credibility because they often contradict Protestant theologians!

DAVID: When does that happen?

TRENT: Here's one. Some Protestant apologists will try to show Peter is not the "rock" in Matthew 16:18, but Protestant theologians think this conclusion is obvious. One of them, D.A. Carson, says, "If it were not for Protestant reactions against extremes of Roman Catholic interpretations, it is doubtful whether many would have taken 'rock' to be anything or anyone other than Peter."[28] Or, you have Protestant apologists saying that Catholic doctrines arose after Constantine even though reputable Protestant historians like J.N.D. Kelly affirm that doctrines like the real presence of Christ in the Eucharist were believed long before that period.[29]

If Catholic apologists are undermined by some Catholic theologians, then the same is true for Protestant apologists who contradict some Protestant theologians.

DAVID: But if these are such good arguments, why aren't these Protestant theologians Catholic?

TRENT: Probably because they have other theological objections they feel have not been answered, or other motives more personal or emotional in nature. I'm not saying these Protestant theologians prove that Catholicism is true. I'm saying that if a contradiction between Catholic apologists and theologians undermines Catholicism, the same thing happens in Protestantism and any belief system.

DAVID: Ah, but there's a crucial difference between the two systems that makes it way easier to be an apologist for Protestantism than to be an apologist for Catholicism.

Safe Bibles and Risky Popes

DAVID: All right, we've talked a lot about what might make you doubt that Christianity is true, but let's get a little more focused and talk about Catholicism. You've got to admit, there's one nice thing about being a Protestant apologist over being a Catholic apologist.

TRENT: What's that?

DAVID: As a Protestant, you have a fixed number of data to defend. It's just a set number of books of the Bible. After studying them, you know all the major objections people will throw at it. It's not as though an atheist will say, "Can you believe that the Bible says *this*?", and you need to turn on the evening news to see what he's talking about.

TRENT: But for Catholics, it's different.

DAVID: Right! You have to deal with everything that was

Does the unchanging nature of the Bible give sola scriptura advocates an advantage?

said by the popes and Church councils for 2,000 years after Christ.

TRENT: So far, the only difficulty you've presented is that Catholic apologists have to do more homework than Protestant apologists. We have more to cover, but the historical objections to Catholicism are pretty well worn. When you read Luther, Calvin, Turrentin Whittaker, Salmon, and modern Protestant apologists, you see similar objections being raised in each work. It's more material to know, but it's not a different kind of problem.

DAVID: Not quite. It's not just that you have to know *more* material to learn; it's that the amount of that material *continues to grow* every day. And with each day that passes, you face the threat of a contradiction that will falsify Catholicism emerging from the mouth of a pope or the bishops. I mean, on more than one occasion, you've had to go online to find out about yet another controversy surrounding Pope Francis's off-the-cuff remarks.

TRENT: They frustrate me, but a comment he says to a reporter or a filmmaker isn't part of Catholic teaching.

DAVID: Just wait till they make their way into an encyclical. As a Catholic, you have to live in fear that Pope Francis, or the next pope after him, or the bishops as a whole, are going to contradict a supposedly infallible teaching of the Church. How long do you think it will be before the pro-gay lobby in the Church gets the Magisterium to teach that sodomy and the marital act are morally equivalent? Or that contraception is

Does the ever-increasing number of magisterial teachings put Catholics at a disadvantage?

Catholics have more truths to defend than Protestants, but overcoming recycled objections is not an insurmountable feat.

not immoral? Once that happens "it's game over, man. Game over!"

What if the pope teaches something heretical tomorrow?

TRENT: By that logic, it's "game over" for most Protestants and even Eastern Orthodox who have accepted the morality of contraception and remarriage after divorce. Why in the world would I leave Catholicism because of a speculative fear that it will embrace these errors in favor of churches or communities that have already embraced them?

Why abandon Catholicism over possible heresy in favor of groups that have already embraced heresy?

DAVID: But you're assuming that they are errors. What if they aren't, and the Catholic Church is wrong about contraception and divorce?

TRENT: We'll get to contraception later, but Jesus made the issue of divorce and remarriage crystal-clear: "Whoever divorces his wife and marries another, commits adultery against her." This teaching may be difficult to live out, but it's not difficult to understand. If Jesus walked out of his own tomb, then I'm going to trust him on this one.

DAVID: Okay, fine. But even if the Protestant apologists are wrong about the content of the book they're sworn to defend, that doesn't change the fixed nature of the book. Protestants get to have a "here's what Jesus said, that's it" attitude. You don't. They don't have to worry about a pope waking up one day and falsifying their whole worldview. They have only the Bible. They know what it says, and that's that. You can see how that would make some people hesitant to take on the baggage associated with Catholicism.

TRENT: Your objection seems to be that an event in the future could falsify Catholicism, but it's far less likely, or maybe even not possible, for a similar future event to falsify Protestantism.

DAVID: More or less.

TRENT: Okay. First, it is possible that Protestantism could be falsified in the future. For example, when atheists ask some Christian apologists, "What would it take for you to give up your faith?", as you did just a moment ago, they often give examples like "a letter from the apostles saying they were frauds" or "archaeologists finding a bone box that says 'Jesus of Nazareth.'" So it's not true that Protestantism is impervious to developments in the future that challenge its essential teachings.

DAVID: But doesn't it unnerve you that it's quite possible you could wake up one morning, get on the internet, and find out that Catholicism is false because Church teaching is now in conflict with itself? The odds of finding something like Jesus' bone box is way, way less likely than the odds of a pope declaring a heresy.

TRENT: But how do you know that? If God exists and he raised Jesus from the dead, then it isn't the case that the odds are lower merely because it's *easier* for the pope to utter heresy than it is for archaeologists to find Jesus' bone box. If the Holy Spirit tells us Jesus rose from the dead, then there is no bone box to be found. Likewise, if the Holy Spirit tells us Christ established the Catholic Church, then the pope will never formally bind the Church to a theological error.

Many Protestant apologists claim that it is possible for Christianity to be falsified.

Is Catholicism more likely to be falsified in the future than Protestantism?

DAVID: Ah, notice you're hedging your bets with phrases like "formally bind the Church to error" instead of just "say something heretical." Protestants don't have to have a million qualifications for the Bible.

If Christ really founded the Catholic Church, then the probability that it will be shown to be false is zero.

Do Catholics arbitrarily create a bunch of qualifications to protect the doctrine of papal infallibility?

Ex Cathedra Statement

A statement made by the pope that is an infallible declaration of dogma. It must be formally made through his authority as the one who sits on the chair (*cathedra*) of St. Peter. Two recent examples of *ex cathedra* statements include the dogmatic definitions of Mary's immaculate conception and her bodily assumption.

TRENT: Once again, that's not true. Even conservative Protestants who fully defend the inerrancy of Scripture say that applies only to the original copies of Scripture. Since those don't exist anymore, it is possible that a copy of a biblical manuscript has an error in it. Fortunately, we have enough copies of the Bible to determine where those copying errors happened. Remember when I wrote a whole chapter about this in my book *Hard Sayings*?

DAVID: So you're saying that just as Protestants believe that the Holy Spirit protects the Bible from asserting errors only under certain conditions, the same is true of the Holy Spirit's protection of the pope: terms and conditions apply.

TRENT: Yes. For example, if the pope is just speaking as a private theologian, then he could be in error. But here's the deal: my confidence in the Church doesn't come from looking *forward* and estimating a low or non-existent probability of a "falsifying event" occurring. It comes from looking *backward* and concluding that Christ established the Church and, because of this fact, he will protect it with the charism of infallibility. Just as a Protestant apologist is confident that the Bible is without errors not because he has solved every difficulty, but because he trusts in the Bible's divine origins, I am confident in the Church because of the good evidence of its divine origins. Without the Church, you wouldn't even be able to know what counts as Scripture to be your fallback authority . . .

If Protestants can qualify what it means for the Bible to be inerrant, then Catholics can qualify what it means for the Church to be infallible.

CHAPTER 13

Canon Fodder

DAVID: The canon question? That old saw? I know you think that's a silver bullet against Protestantism, but Protestants do have some good responses to it.

TRENT: Like what?

DAVID: The Jews didn't have the Catholic Church before Jesus, but they knew what the canon of Scripture was. Jesus even held them accountable for knowing the scriptures. How do you explain that?

TRENT: What do you mean, they knew "the canon of scripture"?

DAVID: Jesus asked them on multiple occasions, "Have you not read . . . ?" Clearly, they must have had a recognized body of Scripture. Otherwise, they could have told Jesus, "Read what? We don't even know what counts as Scripture because we don't have a pope to tell us!"

TRENT: The problem with this argument is that scholars agree that different schools of Jewish thought had different views on which books were inspired. You had the Sadducees and Samaritans with a very restricted view, possibly just the Pentateuch (or the first five books of the Bible), and the Pharisees and Essenes with bigger canons. In some cases, their canons were larger than what modern Jews accept. I doubt that Protestants want the canon of Scripture to be so varied today.

Canon of Scripture

Canon comes from a Greek word that means "rule." In the context of Scripture, canon refers to those writings that the faithful know to be the inspired word of God.

DAVID: But nobody told Jesus, "Sorry, Rabbi, I know you say I'm contradicting this part of the Bible, but guess what: nobody even knows what books belong in the Bible." Jesus held men accountable to the scriptures, so they had to know what *the scriptures* are.

TRENT: I hear this argument a lot, so I'd like specifics. Where did he hold men accountable? To which verses?

DAVID: He said things like "Do you not know the scriptures?" and "You are wrong because you do not know the scriptures."

TRENT: What's interesting is that Jesus seems to cite Scripture based on the particular opponents he's dealing with. For example, when Jesus is talking to the Pharisees, he cites Psalm 118 to say he is the stone the builders rejected. He also cites the prophets to say living water will flow from him, as he does in John 7:38. But when Jesus

If Jews before Christ knew what qualified as Scripture without the Catholic Magisterium, why do Christians today need the Church?

Different Jewish schools of thought had different canons, which is a state of affairs that nearly all Protestants would not accept for the Church.

speaks to the Sadducees on the resurrection of the dead, he cites Exodus 3:14, which is nowhere near as strong a proof of the resurrection as Daniel's description of the dead rising to everlasting life (12:2).

DAVID: Are you saying Jesus accommodated the different canons?

TRENT: It's certainly possible that he did. It could also be the case that the boundaries of the canon for Jews was fuzzy. Jesus could cite the Psalms, for example, because even Jews who had a restricted canon still had high respect for them.

But let's get back to my main point: unless you want the Protestant canon to be just as fuzzy, then you need an authority to authoritatively declare what is and isn't Scripture.

DAVID: Okay, if you say we can't know the contents of the canon with infallible certainty unless we have an infallible authority like the Church to tell us, then you've merely kicked the can down the road: where do we get our infallible certainty that the Church has this infallible authority without *some other* infallible authority to tell us we can trust the Church? If you say we can just trust the Church as a kind of foundational assumption, then why can't Protestants do the same thing with the Bible?

TRENT: I'll be honest: I've never really liked arguments based on *infallible certainty*—or at least, the kind of argument that tries to exclude all subjective judgments from our assessments of Christianity. I agree that, at the end of the day, each of us has to use his own judgment in

If Jesus held men accountable to Scripture, then wouldn't they have to have infallible knowledge of what constituted Scripture?

If we can't know what the Bible is without an infallible Church, then what infallible authority proves the Church to us?

order to determine what is supposed to be a Christian's ultimate authority.

DAVID: Right, so if you are allowed to use your own private judgment of Scripture and history to determine that the Church is that infallible authority, why can't Protestants use *their* private judgment of Scripture and history to determine that these particular books are an infallible authority?

> Could a non-infallible Church give us an infallible canon?

TRENT: They can. I just think any reasoning they would take to get to that conclusion will be less persuasive than the route I've taken by believing that the apostles' teaching authority continued to exist in the form of a Church with a visible, enduring hierarchy.

DAVID: Why can't Protestants just say the canon is an apostolic truth passed down through non-authoritative means? Just because the Church got the canon right, that doesn't mean it's right about everything else it teaches.

TRENT: But how do you know they "got it right"? For example, without relying on the Church's authority, why should I believe that the Gospel of Mark is inspired Scripture even though it 1) never claims to be Scripture and 2) wasn't written by an apostle?

DAVID: Paul says Luke's Gospel is Scripture (1 Tim. 5:18), so even non-apostles could write Scripture.

TRENT: Paul calls one verse in Luke's Gospel Scripture. He never says anything about Luke having written an inspired Gospel. But even if he did, Paul never mentions Mark as having written Scripture. No one in the New

The only commonality among the canonized books is that the early Church eventually accepted them.

Testament does. And you get similar problems with apostolic writings that don't mention Jesus, like 3 John and Paul's letter to Philemon. Why should we believe they are Scripture?

DAVID: Because the apostles wrote them.

TRENT: Was everything the apostles wrote inspired Scripture? If Paul gave Timothy a grocery list, should that be in the Bible?

DAVID: Obviously not.

TRENT: It sounds obvious, but why do we treat the 335 Greek words Paul wrote to Philemon about an escaped slave as Scripture instead of as just part of Paul's personal correspondence?

DAVID: Well, the Church saw a reason to keep copying this letter, so the Church must have valued it as more than personal correspondence.

TRENT: Hmmm . . . it seems as though we're back to the Church helping us understand what is Scripture.

DAVID: Fine. I agree that apostolic authorship is neither a necessary nor a sufficient condition for something being an inspired writing. But you still aren't in a position to say Protestants have no foundation for knowing the canon of Scripture.

TRENT: Why not?

DAVID: Because the *Catechism* says, "Faith is certain. It is more certain than all human knowledge because it is founded on the very word of God who cannot lie"

(157). Why can't a Protestant tell you, "I know by faith that these books are the word of God, and I don't need any Church to tell me that is the case"?

TRENT: By that logic, why can't a Mormon say, "I know by faith that the Book of Mormon is true"?

DAVID: Because God won't lead someone to believe a false text like the Book of Mormon. But you and I agree that the Protestant canon of Scripture is the word of God, so there's no reason God couldn't reveal that to someone through the gift of faith apart from the Church's declaration.

TRENT: But if God won't lead someone to believe a false canon, then why would he lead Protestants to believe that the Bible only has sixty-six books and exclude the inspired deuterocanonical books of Scripture like Wisdom and Tobit?

Ultimately, this subjective criterion for what counts as Scripture can't distinguish among competing subjective claims of authority. That's why I agree with St. Augustine, who said, "For my part, I should not believe the gospel except as moved by the authority of the Catholic Church."[30]

Why can't Protestants simply say "the certainty of faith" guarantees they know what is Scripture apart from the judgment of the Magisterium?

CHAPTER 14

Mary: Quite Contrary

Is Mary often a "final hurdle" for converts to Catholicism?

DAVID: I know that some of the Marian dogmas were among the last things you accepted before your conversion, so maybe that will give us fertile ground to explore lingering doubts.

TRENT: They can be difficult for some converts, especially for those who come from forms of evangelicalism that are somewhat hostile to veneration of Mary. That's not where I came from, but the dogmas did present difficulties before I understood the nature of true veneration of Mary and the saints.

Do Catholics practice Mariology or Mariolatry?

DAVID: But when you look at how some Catholics praise Mary, it goes far beyond veneration. It's adoration. It's worship as if she were some kind of goddess.

TRENT: How do you know that?

DAVID: They parade statues of her like idols and pray to

her alone, as if she were the only one who can save them from their sins.

TRENT: I'm willing to grant that some Catholic cultures have illicitly joined veneration of Mary with indigenous goddess worship. In the fourth century, St. Epiphanius condemned the heretical Collyridians for offering sacrifices to Mary similar to what pagans offered goddesses in their temples. And sure, there are examples of similar behavior even today. But in these cases, the faithful have strayed from true devotion to Mary, which leads us to offering our highest worship to God alone.

It's not just a few excited laymen. Even the saints seem to flirt with Marian idolatry.

Syncretism

In the broad sense, refers to the merging of ideas between cultures. While this is not always wrong, some syncretism replaces Catholic truths with false teachings from human culture. This includes worshipping Mary as being divine and especially as the goddess of some folk mythology.

DAVID: Not so fast . . . it's not just overly pious laymen who take things with Mary too far. Consider St. Alphonsus Liguori. He's a Doctor of the Church, one of the highest honors a saint can receive, and here are some of the ridiculous things he said about Mary:

> If God is angry with a sinner, and Mary takes him under her protection, she withholds the avenging arm of her son, and saves him . . . to Jesus, as a judge, it belongs also to punish; but mercy alone belongs to the Blessed Virgin as a patroness. Meaning,

that we more easily find salvation by having recourse to the mother than by going to the son.[31]

This is blasphemy, plain and simple.

TRENT: These words make me uncomfortable. I won't sugarcoat it. However, our feelings aren't the best guide for determining what's true. Let's think this through together.

DAVID: "Come, let us reason together" (Isa. 1:18), you might say.

TRENT: Right, so let me start with a confession. Sometimes I'm jealous of Catholics who have more freedom than I do when it comes to speaking about our faith.

DAVID: What? You feel muzzled?

> ### Dulia
>
> A Latin term designating veneration and respect given the highest of God's creatures, such as the saints and the Blessed Virgin Mary. It stands in contrast to *latria*, which is the honor and worship due to God alone. St. Thomas Aquinas said worship of God "belongs to latria" and that *latria* "differs from the reverence which we pay to certain excellent creatures; this belongs to dulia." Trent's argument is essentially that Mary can be given lofty praise for being the mother of God, but this praise is not latria, so it isn't idolatry.

TRENT: Sometimes I feel like a defense attorney, and my client is a husband who was falsely accused of murdering

We should fairly interpret religious devotion and not look for easy ways to accuse to someone of heresy.

Those who spend their time refuting objections can be jealous of those who spend their time in rapturous devotion.

his wife. The husband tells his friends exactly how he feels, and he doesn't worry about using exaggerated language to emphasize his love for his wife. But in court, I don't have that same liberty of speech. I have to speak with exact precision so that the other side doesn't use my words against the Faith. Sometimes it's exhausting. I wish I could be the one who gets carried away in his poetic devotion, but that's not how I'm called to serve the body of Christ.

DAVID: So you're saying Alphonsus is just some love-drunk spouse getting carried away with his words? I thought he was an intellectual giant in the Church.

TRENT: I'm saying we should interpret people in the most charitable way possible. This includes interpreting praise of Mary that wasn't meant to be read in the context of something like a debate about Marian dogmas. It also means not leaving out crucial context and other things the person did say.

Mariolatry

A figure of speech referring to the sin of idolatry, or giving divine worship to something other than God, being committed during illicit worship of the Virgin Mary. Often contrasted with the study of Marian theology, or *Mariology*.

DAVID: Whatever do you mean?

TRENT: Take the quote from Alphonsus you mentioned: "We more easily find salvation by having recourse to the mother than by going to the son." You left out what

Many
writings of
the saints
that seem
to be
examples of
Mariolatry
leave out
the saint's
disavowal of
such ideas.

The
Church's
teaching on
Mary should
be examined
based on
magisterial
documents
such as the
Catechism,
not on the
writings
of some
Church
Fathers and
theologians.

he said next: "not as if Mary was more powerful than her son to save us, for we know that Jesus Christ is our only Savior, and that he alone by his merits has obtained and obtains salvation for us."

DAVID: It doesn't matter. What Alphonsus goes on to say undoes his qualification:

> But it is for this reason: that when we have recourse to Jesus, we consider him at the same time as our judge, to whom it belongs to chastise ungrateful souls, and therefore the confidence necessary to be heard may fail us but when we go to Mary, who has no other office than to compassionate us as mother of mercy, and to defend us as our advocate, our confidence is more easily established, and is often greater.[32]

TRENT: Alphonsus is saying Jesus has the ability to damn us for all eternity, and Mary has no such ability. Mary's sole mission in the Church is to lead people to her son, Jesus Christ.

But ultimately, this is a red herring. What is up for debate is what the Church teaches about Mary, not how different theologians have described Mary's role in our salvation.

DAVID: All right! How about the Church's teaching of Mary being *co-redemptrix* or *mediatrix of all graces*? That sounds like replacing Christ to me.

TRENT: The Church does not teach these titles dogmatically, but they have been popular among some theologians, and they can be understood in an orthodox way. Once again, the principle of charity should be used here. Mary *cooperated* with our redemption by freely consenting to be the means for Christ to come into the world.

Marian Dogmas

These are truths about Mary the Church has infallibly defined, and so no one may deny their appropriateness. These include *mother of God*, *ever-virgin*, *immaculately conceived*, and *assumed into heaven*.

DAVID: I still don't like the term.

TRENT: You're not alone. Even theologians and popes have expressed discomfort with it, but the principle of charity should guide us when we read any document, especially the writings of the saints or the Magisterium. Protestants give the same charity to the Bible when it says eyebrow-raising things like "in my flesh I complete what is lacking in Christ's afflictions for the sake of his body, that is, the Church" (Col. 1:24). They don't take Paul to mean that he is some kind of *co-redeemer* who is making up for a deficiency on the cross!

DAVID: Fair enough.

TRENT: So when it comes to *mediatrix*, I would say that Mary, like all the saints in heaven, prays to lead us closer to her son. We mediate for one another whenever we pray for the needs of someone else, but we can do that only through the one mediatorship of Christ (1 Tim.

Co-redemptrix refers to Mary cooperating with God to bring about our redemption, not her being equally responsible for our redemption.

In 1 Corinthians 3:9, Paul says we are God's "fellow workers"—or, in Greek, *synergoi*, which is where we get the word *synergy*.

2:5). The *Catechism* says, "Taken up to heaven she did not lay aside this saving office [of spiritual motherhood] but by her manifold intercession continues to bring us the gifts of eternal salvation. . . . Therefore the Blessed Virgin is invoked in the Church under the titles of advocate, helper, benefactress, and *mediatrix*" (969).

CHAPTER 15

Mary: Ever-Virgin, Immaculate, and Assumed?

DAVID: I still feel as though you're bending over backward to explain something that shouldn't have to be explained. If you have to give a lengthy explanation in order to justify something, maybe you should question whether it's justifiable at all.

TRENT: That's just anti-intellectualism. I'm sure our Protestant brothers and sisters would agree that a "lengthy explanation" may be needed to help a Muslim understand that the Trinity isn't polytheism, but that doesn't falsify the Trinity just because the explanation is longer than a tweet.

If Mary is the mother of God, why isn't Herod the king of God?

DAVID: Let's try explaining the Marian dogmas, then. I admit that the first one seems obvious: if Jesus is God, and Mary is his mother, then Mary is the mother of God. Although I do wonder why you don't call Herod *the king of God* since if he was the king ruling over Jesus, then he was the king ruling over God.

TRENT: Christians don't do that because there is no direct relationship between Herod being king and Jesus being God. However, there is a direct relationship between Mary being a mother and Jesus being God: Mary bore God in her womb, and through her, he received his humanity.

DAVID: And it's not confusing to say God has a mother?

TRENT: If God becomes man, it makes sense to ask how he became man, since he could have made himself a human body from nothing. But Galatians 4:4 tells us, "When the time had fully come, God sent forth his Son, born of woman, born under the law." If you deny that Mary is the mother of God, then you are denying that Jesus was divine throughout his whole earthly life.

> *Mary directly contributed to the incarnation of God the Son. Herod did not.*

> *Denying Mary's divine maternity leads to denying Jesus' divinity.*

Dogma

A truth of the Faith that the Church has infallibly defined as being part of divine revelation or as being a necessary fact related to divine revelation. For example, the Church has infallibly defined that Mary is *Theotokos*, which means "God-bearer" or "Mother of God." A *dogmatic fact* that can be known with equal certainty is that the ecumenical council of Ephesus (A.D. 431), which defined Mary to be *Theotokos*, was a valid ecumenical council.

DAVID: But aren't you concerned that the other dogmas aren't as obvious? You feel pretty confident defending Mary as *Theotokos* to a Protestant, but Mary being ever-virgin, immaculately conceived, and assumed into heaven starts to get into shakier territory.

TRENT: If someone believes that Jesus is God, then the conclusion Mary is the mother of God follows with absolute certainty. The other Marian dogmas don't follow from Mary being *Theotokos* with this same high level of certainty, but they are fitting, and they make sense of all the available evidence.

DAVID: But let's be real with each other. If you just read the Bible without any Catholic presuppositions, would you honestly walk away saying Mary was ever-virgin, protected from all sin since her conception, and assumed into heaven?

TRENT: Many Protestant Reformers read the Bible with active hostility and resistance to any "Catholic presuppositions" they might have had, and they agreed that Mary was ever-virgin. In 1533, a Lutheran named Hermann Busche defended infant baptism, saying that even though it's not in the Bible, there are many things "not mentioned in the Bible that are still perfectly acceptable. For example, the perpetual virginity of Mary."[33] This was also the position of nearly all the Church Fathers and early Christian authors save for a few outliers like Helvidius. When you divorce the written word of God from the word of God in Sacred Tradition, you lose a sure foundation for interpreting the text, and that can lead to all kinds of bizarre theologies.

> Not every Marian dogma has equal amounts of evidence in its favor, but they all have sufficient evidence to justify belief.

> Early Protestants did not believe that Mary's perpetual virginity was unbiblical.

DAVID: Or it can lead to bizarre theology because of the addition of nebulous "traditions." The problem with these dogmas is that even the Church Fathers don't agree, so *tradition* seems to be you just picking and choosing from among them. For example, Chrysostom accused Mary of acting with "superfluous vanity," and Origen believed she sinned.[34]

Do Catholics "pick and choose" traditions in order to justify Marian dogmas?

The overall direction of the Church Fathers' writings is evidence of Sacred Tradition becoming more formally known in the Church.

Sacred Tradition

The unchanging word of God that is given to the Church in an unwritten form. It is witnessed in the Church's liturgy and the writings of the Church Fathers (CCC 78), but it is not identical to those things. The Council of Trent taught that "this truth and rule [of the gospel] are contained in written books and in unwritten traditions."

TRENT: Well, the Church doesn't consider Origen a Church Father because of certain heretical beliefs he held. The proper term for him is an *ecclesiastical writer*.

DAVID: Don't dodge the question. Nobody denies that Origen was a giant of Christian apologetics.

TRENT: He was, and we shouldn't throw him out, but it's good to be precise in our terms. Anyway, whether we're talking about Origen or John Chrysostom or anyone else, for something to belong to Apostolic Tradition, it doesn't need to be uniformly believed in the early Church. Instead, we need to view the trajectory of these doctrines as they developed in the life of the Church.

DAVID: That sounds like an excuse for the fact that you

can't find early evidence for either the Immaculate Conception or the Assumption.

TRENT: Well, let me ask you this: what is the earliest reference to Adam's fault passing on original sin to his descendants?

DAVID: Augustine, but you can find Church Fathers affirming the idea of original sin before him.

TRENT: And you can also find Fathers like Justin Martyr and Clement of Alexandria, who say Adam's sin was an example of our sinful behavior but not the *cause* of it. It seems as if the Fathers don't agree on a crucial Christian doctrine.

DAVID: Well, we have to look at . . .

TRENT: . . . the trajectory of the doctrine? I agree, and by the time of Augustine and the Second Council of Orange (529), the doctrine of original sin became much more firmly established, especially as the Church faced the heresy of Pelagianism. We see something similar with the Patristic understanding of Mary's sinlessness, which even Protestant historians recognize among the Fathers.

> Some doctrines that Protestants agree with, such as original sin, also do not become explicit until centuries after the apostles.

Pelagianism

Heresy named after the priest Pelagius, who claimed that human beings could attain salvation through their own merits apart from the grace of God. It denied that Adam's sin made humans incapable of approaching God through their own sinful wills.

DAVID: All this trajectory stuff just obscures the fact that Catholic apologists have to piece the evidence for their dogmas together like a jigsaw puzzle where you jam pieces to make them fit. In this case, you try to make the Fathers be a witness to your own ideas about Sacred Tradition.

TRENT: Remember when I said evidence is like money? Would I like universal acknowledgment of the Marian dogmas among the Fathers to be at the same level as the Real Presence or baptismal regeneration in the early Church? Of course I would. But just as we see a trajectory that moves on other subjects, like the canon of Scripture or the inner workings of the Trinity, we see something similar in Mary going from being called *all-holy* and *incorruptible* to being declared free from sin and then *immaculately conceived*. This makes more sense than a trajectory that moves from Mary being considered sinless by many early Christians to her being "a sinner just like us."

DAVID: Some of this "trajectory" just seems to come out of thin air, though. You're not going to find the dogma of the Assumption before the fifth century, and nobody before that time thought the woman "clothed with the sun" in heaven in Revelation 12 was Mary assumed into heaven.

TRENT: Some early Christians also thought the entire book of Revelation wasn't canonical, so this absence of evidence doesn't prove much. One Protestant author says, "It is not surprising, therefore, to find that Marian interpretation of Revelation 12 begins in the fifth century, after the New Testament canon is fixed."[35] Also, apocryphal works like the *Book of Mary's Repose* may reliably transmit traditions about the Assumption that date to the second and third centuries.

DAVID: What about early Church Fathers who wrote about people being assumed into heaven? None of them mentions Mary, even though writing about that subject would have been the perfect opportunity for them to do so.

TRENT: You should be careful with making arguments from silence. I've checked those citations, and in many of those cases, it wouldn't make sense for the Fathers to mention Mary because they are talking only about events in the Old Testament. Or they talk about God delivering people from death, but the dogma of the Assumption doesn't definitively teach that Mary died—only that her body and soul were taken up to heaven.[36] Mythicists make the same argument against Jesus' existence because Paul doesn't cite Jesus' miracles or explicit teachings, even when they think it would make sense for Paul to mention those things. So this isn't a path I recommend going down for your argument.

Why don't we see dogmas like Mary's assumption in patristic evidence that talks about the concept of assumptions in general?

Arguments from silence are weak if they rely on faulty assumptions of where we would expect evidence for certain doctrines.

Argument from Silence

The claim that if X were true, then evidence Y would exist. Since we do not see evidence Y, it follows that X is not true. While sometimes valid, these arguments can rely on faulty assumptions. These include incorrectly saying some kinds of evidence must always accompany certain claims or not taking into account our inability to find the absent evidence. (For example, evidence in ancient documents may have been lost over time.)

DAVID: All I'll say is that you're building a really flimsy popsicle-stick bridge for these dogmas.

Do Catholics believe only what the Church teaches and not care about evidence?

TRENT: That might be true if I were trying to prove this doctrine from Scripture and historical arguments alone. But I'm Catholic, so I don't have to do that. If Christ founded the Church, then I can trust what it says about the deposit of faith.

DAVID: *Sola ecclesia.* If the Church says it, I believe it, and that settles it. And I thought you were opposed to anti-intellectualism.

TRENT: Each of us sets up a standard of evidence that governs what we will and won't believe. I could say the same to you: what determines if a Christian should believe in a certain doctrine? Is it *sola scriptura*? Too bad *sola scriptura* is not in the Bible. Maybe *sola scriptura* and "early Patristic evidence"? But who determines the cutoff year for a belief to have arisen early enough to count as having sufficient Patristic evidence? In fact, your complaints about certain Marian dogmas and their Patristic witness reek of a double-standard.

DAVID: How so?

TRENT: Your argument seems to be that if the Assumption and the Immaculate Conception were apostolic teachings, they would figure more prominently in the early Church Fathers.

DAVID: You bet.

TRENT: But many Protestant doctrines, such as *sola scriptura*, the denial of baptismal regeneration, and the impossibility of losing salvation are also absent from the early Church Fathers.

DAVID: But Protestants don't get their doctrines from the Fathers; they get them from the Bible. And they will say those doctrines are evident in Scripture alone.

TRENT: The problem is that the original argument still works against them. If these Protestant doctrines really were in Scripture, and are not a false interpretation of Scripture, then we'd expect the Fathers to be a witness to them as well. But since we don't, this provides strong evidence they aren't in Scripture at all. Any doubts I have about the patristic pedigree of some secondary Catholic dogmas is outweighed by the complete absence of the primary doctrines of the Reformation from those same sources.

The absence of fundamental Protestant doctrines in the Fathers is fatal.

CHAPTER 16

What About Abortion and Euthanasia?

TRENT: There is no way you're going to get me to doubt the Church's teaching on abortion.

DAVID: Are you sure?

TRENT: Yes. This one has always seemed obvious to me, even before my conversion. The philosophical arguments are strong, and the pictures of dead babies seal the deal. I don't know how you're going to shake me.

DAVID: Well, let's look at those arguments. You believe that abortion is wrong because it kills an innocent person.

TRENT: Correct—not just a human being, but a *person*, an individual member of a rational kind. Personhood is not about what you can do, but about what you are.

Persons include infants, fetuses, you, me, conscious aliens, non-rational infant aliens . . .

DAVID: . . . *non-rational infant aliens?*

TRENT: Imagine a "baby Yoda."

DAVID: Okay, got it.

TRENT: . . . angels—they are all persons, even though their functional abilities vary considerably.

DAVID: Even a human being in a persistent vegetative state who will never be conscious again?

TRENT: Yes, he is a person even if he will never again function like a person.

DAVID: But that means if you take this person off life support, you will have murdered him. Are you really saying taking a person in a vegetative state off life support is an act of murder?

TRENT: No. We both agree it's not wrong to take someone who has experienced total brain death off life support, like a heart-lung machine. We just have different reasons for why we think it's okay to do this.

DAVID: My reason is that you aren't killing a person when you do that; you are just letting that person's body die.

TRENT: For you, it isn't wrong because we aren't dealing with a *person.* I, on the other hand, don't think it's wrong because we aren't dealing with *murder.* Taking a brain-dead person off life support isn't unjust killing; it's a morally permissible way of letting someone die.

Is it wrong to kill persons who will never function like persons again? Are they still "persons"?

Taking a brain-dead person off life support isn't murder, but both sides disagree about why.

DAVID: All right, but what about a feeding tube? Do you think someone whose brain will never function again should have a feeding tube for decades of unconscious existence?

Not every dying person needs food and water, but it's always wrong to cause death by depriving someone of food and water.

TRENT: Every human being, no matter his disability, has the right to food and water if that is necessary for his survival. You might refrain from feeding some people because they're about to die (like when it's painful for them to digest food), but it's always cruel to purposefully starve someone to death.

DAVID: So you're saying the person's family, or society, needs to pay for someone who will never be conscious again to just lie in a bed for fifty years? How does that make any sense? The person is already basically dead. You're just keeping tissue alive for the sake of keeping tissue alive.

Saying some people aren't valuable because of their disability echoes the rationale of the worst atrocities in human history.

TRENT: Have you ever heard of *Lebensunwertes Leben*?

DAVID: No, but I've got a feeling you're going to tell me what it means.

TRENT: It's German for "life unworthy of life." That's what you're calling people in vegetative states. But where do you draw the line? What about someone with a severe mental handicap who barely functions above the level of an infant? Or a quadriplegic?

DAVID: I draw the line at those who want to live. If they don't even have a desire to live, then why think it's wrong to just let them die already?

TRENT: So if a quadriplegic wants to die because he

thinks he is "life unworthy of life," you'd let him kill himself?

Is abortion okay if both the mother and child will die otherwise?

DAVID: Sure.

TRENT: What about the teenager who's depressed because his girlfriend dumped him?

DAVID: That's different, because he still has his whole life ...

TRENT: Ah! So it's not just about people who want to live or don't. You do make a distinction between someone irrationally killing himself (like a depressed teenager) and someone rationally doing it because, in your opinion, his life is not worth living. That seems really dangerous to me.

DAVID: What seems really dangerous to me is a pro-life ethic that says it is always wrong to kill an unborn child, no matter what. What if a woman is twelve weeks pregnant and needs an abortion or else she will die? Under your view, it would better for both the mother and the child to die than to do at least something to save one of them.

TRENT: Look, every view in ethics that is consistent will lead to tough conclusions. Let's take your example. Your ethical principle is, "It's okay to kill one person who will die anyway in order to save the life of another person." What if Bob needs a new heart, and a terminally ill patient named Frank has the only match? Would Bob have the right to kill Frank and take his heart because Frank was going to die anyway?

DAVID: I think you need to own this, though: in some

cases, you'd let the mother and baby die when you could at least save one of them. That's monstrous.

Utilitarianism

A system of ethics that says an act is good if it promotes the most *utility* or well-being. Trent is arguing that David's utilitarianism leads to morally repugnant conclusions like murdering the innocent in order to save lives.

TRENT: In some rare cases, two people might die because morality demands that a third party not commit murder. It is tragic when extremely rare situations happen and it is physically or even morally impossible to save someone's life. But when we make ethical judgments based on emotions instead of solid principles, that's where we can end up with monstrous conclusions. You're basically arguing for *utilitarianism*, and if I just press a tiny bit, you can see the horrors that result from seeing people as a means to promote utility instead of as ends in themselves.

DAVID: Your pro-life ethic treats people as means, since women become involuntary organ donors. Frank doesn't have to donate any part of his body in order to save Bob's life, so why does the pregnant women have to donate her body in order to keep a fetus alive?

TRENT: Come on. If you engage in an act known for causing people to come into existence who need the use of another person's body for life support, then you owe those people assistance because of the position in which you've put them.

DAVID: All right, then suppose I know that if I become pregnant, my child will one day need a bone marrow transplant from me when she is twenty-five. Am I obligated to give her bone marrow because I know that in the future, she will become dependent on my body?

If I cause someone to depend on my body, then do I have to give an organ to him later on if he needs it to survive?

TRENT: No. Refusing to donate an organ involves letting someone die, whereas abortion involves the active killing of a healthy person. Also, my kidneys were made for my body, so it's extraordinary (and therefore not obligatory) to donate them to someone else.

DAVID: Why can't a pregnant woman make the same argument? If her uterus is only for children she wants, then she doesn't have to let an unwanted child use it. But if her uterus is for any child who needs it, then why can't your kidneys be for any sick person who needs them?

There is a natural use of organs that is obligatory, which includes an unborn child's use of the uterus in the body in which he was conceived.

TRENT: Those aren't the only two options. A woman's uterus is "for" the children she conceives, regardless of whether she wants to care for them.

DAVID: What about surrogate mothers? By your logic, they'd have a right to abort because they didn't conceive the children they carry.

TRENT: Well, I think surrogacy is evil and shouldn't be allowed in the first place.

DAVID: That doesn't answer the question.

TRENT: I'd say a surrogate should not be allowed to abort because she's legally agreed to carry the child. It would be the same as holding a wet nurse who agreed to feed a newborn legally responsible for using her body to sustain that child.

Do embryos who weren't conceived within a particular woman have a right to reside in that woman's body if they need it to survive?

DAVID: Then your view allows for abortion if a woman is forced to carry an embryo that is implanted within her against her will that is not related to her.

TRENT: I don't think so. She may be responsible to care for that child, just as a rural nursing mother who discovers an abandoned baby might be obligated to nurse that child. But even if my argument didn't work in that one case, it would still show that 99.9999 percent of abortions are immoral. I'd say that is a spectacularly strong ethical argument!

Are bodi-ly-rights arguments for abortion not just wrong, but self-contra-dictory?

Also, here's the problem I have with these "right to refuse" bodily-autonomy arguments. You say, at least for the sake of the argument, that the fetus has a right to life.

DAVID: Correct.

TRENT: But not a right to reside in his mother's body.

DAVID: Also correct.

TRENT: What does it mean that the fetus has a right to life?

DAVID: It means it is a person you can't unjustly kill.

TRENT: And how would you unjustly kill a fetus versus justly killing him?

DAVID: Well . . .

TRENT: See, there's your problem. For adults, the right to life usually entails just leaving them alone. Don't stab, shoot, or strangle them. But for very young children, leaving them alone is what kills them. That's what violates their right to life—and so, since they are persons, this gives them the right to demand that other people care for them. You may say the fetus is a person, but if you don't also say another person has moral duties toward this fetus, then he is really a person in name only. The only way the unborn can truly be a person, a child, is if others also have a duty to feed and shelter him—namely, the people who brought the child into existence.

It's incoherent to say that unborn children have a right to life but no right to the things they need to live.

DAVID: I guess you were right in your confidence about being disabused of your pro-life intuitions.

CHAPTER 17

The Hardest Cases

DAVID: I think one of the biggest problems with your Catholicism is that it works in theory but not in the nitty-gritty aspects of life. For example, I need you to do something for me . . .

TRENT: What's that?

DAVID: Imagine there is a nice, youngish mother standing next to me. Thirty-five years old, and has three kids. She has a medical condition that makes her, let's say, prone to strokes or heart attacks, and the doctors have told her that if she gets pregnant again, she'll die.

TRENT: Okay . . .

DAVID: I want you to look her in the eyes and tell her she can't have sex with her husband anymore because the Church says so.

TRENT: That's not what the Church teaches.

DAVID: So she's supposed to gamble her life with natural family planning? The method that "always works" because unintended pregnancies are just "blessed surprises"?

Can an apologist deliver the truth even when it hurts?

TRENT: It's possible to practice NFP to avoid having children, but yes, there is always a chance you'll conceive a child.

DAVID: According to you, she can't morally use contraceptives, even though it will kill her to conceive a child. She isn't even saying "no" to life; God did that for her by afflicting her with this condition.

Contraceptives aren't a risk-free approach to preventing high-risk pregnancies, either.

TRENT: She is saying she does not want children to proceed from her sexual union. It may be a more serious reason than something related to financial or emotional health, but it differs only in degree and not in kind from the typical reasons contraceptives are used. Also, contraceptives aren't a hundred percent effective, either, so she'd still be taking a risk using birth control.

DAVID: Fine. What about a hysterectomy?

TRENT: That would be an immoral form of sterilization since, given your brief description of the case, her uterus seems to be perfectly healthy. She seems to have some other medical condition exacerbated by pregnancy.

DAVID: I want you to look at her and tell her the blunt truth—"you can never safely experience marital intimacy again"—and see how much anguish this will cause her. You're good at reciting the correct answers, but one

The critic
is focusing
only on
harms in
this life
instead of
the greater
spiritual
harm caused
by sin.

day, you'll see that most people don't buy those answers when they have to be paid for in real life. They stop believing in the Church when you have to actually look at someone you love and tell her the heartless truth.

TRENT: The truth can't be "heartless"; only people can have that quality.

DAVID: But doesn't a deep part of you want to say, "Ah, well, it's really not a big deal. One little surgery, and this woman can have her life back again"?

TRENT: Yes, a part of me does instinctively want to say that. Sometimes I feel discouraged because even I, a Catholic apologist, have secular knee-jerk reactions on occasion to tough issues where I just want what makes everyone happy. But Jeremiah 17:9 says, "The heart is deceitful above all things, and desperately corrupt; who can understand it?" That's why you and I need to get an "eternal perspective."

DAVID: Come again?

TRENT: When you bring up these hard cases, the only harm you recognize are the pains on this side of the veil. You're ignoring what sin does to us.

DAVID: Is it really a sin, though, for her to have a simple surgery?

TRENT: A hysterectomy is anything but "simple." Our culpability might change, given many personal factors, but purposefully destroying healthy organs is mutilation. And as I said before, where will your "compassion" end? Some people get married, and an accident happens that leaves their spouse unable to have sexual intercourse ever again.

DAVID: Well, maybe divorce isn't so bad in some exceptional cases.

TRENT: By whose standard? When it comes to divorce, this one is almost as obvious to me as abortion. Jesus said, "Whoever divorces his wife and marries another, commits adultery against her; and if she divorces her husband and marries another, she commits adultery" (Mark 10:11-12).

DAVID: But honestly, what do you tell the woman whose husband runs off with his secretary, leaves her with the kids, and now she can't even get remarried to a nice guy that could put her family back together again?

TRENT: I would say, "I'm sorry for what you are going through. I can't even imagine how difficult it must be." I would pray for her and try to reassure her about the crosses she is carrying . . .

DAVID: Oh, yes, it's easy to encourage people to carry impossible crosses when you barely have any of your own to carry.

TRENT: I do feel bad about that.

DAVID: You do?

TRENT: I have struggles . . . but nothing like the examples you've brought up. I'm not sure I have enough credibility to encourage people in these tough cases . . . but that doesn't mean I'm wrong. In fact, I'm going to turn the tables on you.

What difficult teaching could survive the critic's "compassion"?

We must be careful when judging whether some things aren't so bad. Not so bad . . . according to us or God?

DAVID: What?

TRENT: When should remarriage after divorce be allowed? What about a couple that just mutually grow apart and don't care what the divorce will do to their kids? Or what about a couple that just refuse to go to counseling to save their marriage? Where do you draw the line? Or does God not care about divorce? Oh wait, he told the prophet Malachi, "I hate divorce" (2:16).

DAVID: I'm not talking about cases like that. I'm just talking about exceptions for the impossibly hard cases.

TRENT: I feel as though you're a theological nightclub bouncer. You're willing to let people into the "exceptions" club if they look as though they've suffered enough, but you're always arbitrarily drawing the line when you say one person's suffering justifies an exception to a moral rule, but another person's doesn't. Why don't you just be honest and say you don't care about the rules God laid down?

DAVID: I can be critical of Catholic morality without endorsing relativism. Oh, and let me just tell you about relativism. When Catholic speakers say, "Oh, no, the world has embraced relativism!", that's so inaccurate. People agree that it's wrong to intentionally hurt other people. We all agree that murder, theft, and rape are wrong. You're the one trying to impose unnecessary burdens on people by saying there are evils that don't involve pain.

TRENT: Like what?

DAVID: Consensual, non-marital sex. Honestly, what is

the big deal when two people's genitals come together as long as they enjoy it?

Is consensual, non-marital sex really so bad if nobody gets hurt?

TRENT: Why stop at two people?

DAVID: Sure, the more, the merrier.

TRENT: Under your view, though, is there such a thing as sexually *disordered* behavior involving consenting adults?

DAVID: As long as they consent, I don't think so.

TRENT: All right. I'm going to have to get gross, because the culture has gone so far down the sexual rabbit hole. What about someone who has sex with the dead body of his spouse?

DAVID: Did the spouse consent before death?

TRENT: Ohhhh . . . kay. Whew . . . how about animals?

DAVID: That's different because animals can't consent to sex.

TRENT: Can animals consent to being killed and eaten?

DAVID: I guess not.

TRENT: So, and as I said, this is gross to contemplate, but if you can eat animals without their consent, then why not have sex with them?

DAVID: Because . . . I don't even know where to begin.

TRENT: You don't know because if you talk about what's *natural*, we need ask why it's natural or unnatural. Sex with animals, or little children, or inanimate objects . . . you know what? It's not even sex.

DAVID: What do you mean? If, well, the parts come together . . . I mean, it could be any genitals.

TRENT: Or genitals and orifices . . .

DAVID: Sure.

TRENT: The problem is that if you define it that crudely, then you can't distinguish mutual masturbation from sexual intercourse. The Catholic view makes more sense: sex, which expresses marital love, refers only to vaginal intercourse. Everything else is "sexual behavior" rather than sex. That means that sexual stimulation using animals, using inanimate objects, self-stimulation, or stimulation between humans of the same sex—none of that is sex.

DAVID: Are you seriously going to compare a loving relationship between a same-sex couple with somebody who engages in "sexual behavior" with an animal?

TRENT: I'm not saying they are the same in every respect. Fornication, adultery, and sodomy all differ in many respects, but they are all wrong because they place the sexual act—or, in the case of sodomy, an imitation of the sexual act—outside of the marital act God created uniting men and women in a *one-flesh* life-giving bond. In fact, one aspect of our culture makes me sure of that: infidelity.

DAVID: I thought infidelity was a sign that our culture was going to hell in a handbasket.

TRENT: Adultery has been around forever, and even though popular sexual morality has changed on issues

If you can eat animals without their consent, then why not have sex with them? If it's unnatural, then what kind of sex is natural for humans?

Sex means vaginal intercourse.

like homosexuality and contraception, there is always a constant drumbeat that infidelity is wrong. But if sex were just about pleasure or "showing love," you wouldn't expect that. You can love lots of different people like family or friends, but sexual love seems by its nature to be ordered to only one other person, and that makes the most sense.

DAVID: This isn't a matter of the nature of *sex*, but rather a matter of the nature of *commitments*. You have to keep your commitments (like marriage), but not necessarily have sex with only one person. Most people today agree with me on that.

TRENT: But this is about what kind of *sexual commitments* we are bound to keep. Most people would think a marriage built on a promise of vegetarianism is asking too much, or at least is idiosyncratic. But nobody bats an eye at the idea that married people (or even people in a publicly defined relationship like dating) commit not to have sex with anyone else.

DAVID: That could just be thousands of years of evolution telling people what sexual behaviors ensure survival of the fittest.

TRENT: People also say, and they may be right, that racism is a product of our evolutionary history that reinforced tribal bonds, but everyone tries really hard to overcome that evolutionary programming. Evolution also programs us to think we must scarf down fast-food cheeseburgers out of a deep-seated genetic need for lots of fat and salt, and we work to overcome that, too. But

Sexually immoral acts can differ in their moral gravity while still being equally outside God's plan for our sexuality.

Widespread condemnation of infidelity is indirect evidence for sex having a intrinsically monogamous purpose.

in this case, many people would say evolution got it right, which seems odd for an unguided process of nature.

Should we trust evolutionary instincts, or is there a higher plan that guides our moral lives?

DAVID: Until polyamory catches on and nobody cares about who sleeps with whom.

TRENT: I try not to make predictions about the future, but I highly doubt that will happen, at least on a large scale. I think the moral law, and especially God's plan for our sexuality, is too deeply ingrained in us. Sexual disorder is common, but even the need to associate masturbation with images of sex shows that people connect the pleasure of orgasm with bodily union. If sex were just for pleasure or "appreciation" of others, then public masturbation might be considered rude, like public nose-picking, but not a crime. Or infidelity might be considered a faux pas rather than a major betrayal. But all of this shows that sex is for something that the mere pleasures of this world cannot entirely explain—something that makes sense only if we have an "eternal perspective."

CHAPTER 18

Paging Gordon Gekko

TRENT: Honestly, it's not the Church's teachings on the "pelvic issues" I struggle with the most. It's the teachings on economics.

DAVID: That would make sense, given your devotion to capitalism. You're basically a reincarnation of Michael J. Fox's "young Reaganite" from that '80s sitcom *Family Ties*.

TRENT: That was a great show! But yeah, there's a reason I co-wrote a book on why Catholics can't be socialists. I wouldn't call myself a Reaganite, but I do think free markets have done tremendous good for the world. For me, economics isn't just an interesting field of study; it's a major way we can carry out works of mercy like caring for the poor.

DAVID: And where did Jesus say we should use free markets to do that?

TRENT: He didn't. Jesus also didn't talk about building hospitals to heal the sick, but I'm glad Christians invented the modern hospital. Just as we don't restrict ourselves to first-century approaches to curing illness, we shouldn't restrict ourselves to first-century approaches to alleviating poverty.

Can Catholics support free markets?

The Catholic Church does not support "unfettered, unconcerned" capitalism.

DAVID: And what is that modern solution? Free markets? Pope Francis said we need to say "'thou shalt not' to an "economy of exclusion and inequality. Such an economy kills. How can it be that it is not a news item when an elderly homeless person dies of exposure, but it is news when the stock market loses two points?" (*Evangelii Gaudium* 45).

TRENT: ::sigh::

DAVID: You seem exasperated.

TRENT: Yes, I am.

DAVID: Why?

TRENT: Because I feel torn in two directions when I listen to the Magisterium teach on economic issues. On the one hand, there are many, many points I completely agree with and wish other defenders of the free market would embrace.

DAVID: Like what?

TRENT: The famous economist Milton Friedman once said companies do not have moral responsibilities; they have only a legal responsibility to follow the law and a financial responsibility to their shareholders.[37] I don't hold that view because Catholic social teaching justifiably exhorts business-owners to carry out all kinds of moral duties toward their employees, consumers, and communities. Now, I disagree with people about how the State should get owners to carry out these duties, but I believe that the duties do exist.

DAVID: Then what's the problem with what the Church teaches?

TRENT: The problem is that, on the other hand, some of what is contained in these magisterial documents is just pablum.

DAVID: Pablum?

TRENT: It's a mushy cereal that's easy for babies to eat. It's also a kind of argument or rhetoric that doesn't say anything of substance—and frankly, that's what I see sometimes in magisterial teaching on economics.

DAVID: So it's pablum to point out that people care more about the stock market losing two points than an elderly person dying of exposure?

TRENT: If the point is that it's wrong to value a few more dollars in retirement over actual human lives, then no, it's a fair point. But if you're saying free markets in and of themselves are an "economy that kills," then that is asinine. Free markets aren't perfect because people aren't perfect. But free markets were the critical factor in dropping global rates of extreme poverty from ninety-four percent in 1820 to less than ten percent today.

Are some Catholic teachings on economics shallow or unhelpful?

Free markets can allow things to exist that can cause harm, but they have been an overall boon to human well-being.

DAVID: Pope Francis has an answer for that, you know. In *Fratelli Tutti*, he says: "The claim that the modern world has reduced poverty is made by measuring poverty with criteria from the past that do not correspond to present-day realities. In other times, for example, lack of access to electric energy was not considered a sign of poverty, nor was it a source of hardship" (21).

Are some political conservatives "cafeteria Catholics" when it comes to Church teaching on economics?

TRENT: Here's what's wrong with that argument . . .

DAVID: Wait!

TRENT: But I was going to . . .

DAVID: Hold on a minute. Don't you see what you're doing? You regularly complain about the "cafeteria Catholics" who refuse to say homosexual orientations are "intrinsically disordered," but now you refuse to accept what the Church teaches about economics. That's the pot calling the kettle a dissenter.

Church teaching on prudential matters should inform Catholics, but it is not as authoritative as pronouncements on faith and morals.

Prudential Judgments

Decisions about what is the best way to pursue the good. These judgments involve the virtue of prudence and Catholics can reasonably disagree about their value.

TRENT: There is a difference between Church teaching on faith and morals and Church teaching on other matters that involve prudential judgments. For example, we must help the poor. That's non-negotiable. But we can disagree about how to help the poor. In *Donum Veritatis*, the Congregation for the Doctrine of the Faith noted that "when it comes to the question of interventions in the prudential order, it could happen that some magisterial documents might not be free from all deficiencies. Bishops and their advisors have not always taken into immediate consideration every aspect or the entire complexity of a question" (24).

If capitalism is bad, what's the alternative?

DAVID: This just seems really suspicious. When it is something you disagree with the Church about, it becomes a prudential judgment, but when you agree with the Church, it's an infallible teaching with which you can beat people over the head.

TRENT: I don't disagree with Church teachings about how we must have a "preferential option for the poor." And I'm all in favor of a fair critique of capitalism. But what I can't stand are vague criticisms of free markets that don't specify what we ought to do instead.

DAVID: Is that what you think the pope has done?

TRENT: Sometimes, yeah. For example, in *Fratelli Tutti*, the pope says the market can't solve every problem, and I agree with that sentiment. But then he says, "It is imperative to have a proactive economic policy directed at promoting an economy that favors productive diversity and business creativity and makes it possible for jobs to be created and not cut" (168).

The problem is, I don't know what that means. All I take from that is, "Yeah, we need more opportunities for job creation," but letting people engage in free markets is the best way to create those things. I don't know . . .

DAVID: You don't know about what?

TRENT: I'm torn. Some of the Magisterium's advice on economics frustrates me, but I also don't want to worship at the altar of extreme "laissez-faire" economics. I feel guilty that I'm not giving enough to the poor when I could be doing more and that we can't always rely on private charity or free markets to help people. I just think economics is a big, complicated issue, and I'm eager to apply the Church's "banner teachings" to it, like subsidiarity or the benefit of private labor unions. But I'm not happy with the concept of free markets constantly being thrown under the bus, given the good they have done.

When does criticism of the Church's positions become unfaithfulness or even apostasy?

Wait! That reminds me . . .

Subsidiarity

A principle in Catholic social teaching that says a higher entity should subside and allow the more local organization to manage a situation whenever possible. For example, local and state governments should address social problems before the federal government if they are able to do so. It is described in Pope Pius XI's encyclical *Quadragesimo Anno* (80).

DAVID: Of what?

TRENT: The thing in *Fratelli Tutti* about measuring poverty in different time periods. It said, "Poverty must always be understood and gauged in the context of the actual opportunities available in each concrete historical period." Yes, it is unjust that people have lack of access to reliable electricity today when so many people have it, and it wasn't unjust 400 years ago, since that technology didn't exist yet. But free markets were what made it possible to lift people out of those conditions.

DAVID: But maybe your faith in free markets is misplaced. Especially damning is that we'd expect Christians in the free market to act with such generosity that there would never be poverty. But that's not what we see.

TRENT: I agree. That really bothers me. In fact, these *meager moral fruits* among the faithful represent some of my biggest concerns . . .

CHAPTER 19

Meager Moral Fruits I

DAVID: So you've saved the best for last, eh?

TRENT: Yeah, this argument is a perplexing one for me. There are aspects of it that make me want to dismiss it outright, but then there are parts of it that stick around in my head and unnerve me.

DAVID: Well, don't keep us in suspense!

TRENT: It's called the argument from meager moral fruits. It basically says: if Christianity is true, then why aren't Christians noticeably more moral than non-Christians? The Christian apologist Ravi Zacharias said a Hindu friend once asked him, "If this conversion you speak about is truly supernatural, why is it not more evident in the lives of so many Christians that I know?" Zacharias said this comment haunted him throughout his ministry. It's especially ironic now that we know that Zacharias was involved in numerous sex scandals.[38]

138

DAVID: It's sort of a variant of the problem of evil, wouldn't you say? But in this case, the evil we wouldn't expect if God did exist is the lack of virtue among so-called believers.

TRENT: That's a decent way to summarize the argument. On the whole, I agree with the major premise that we would expect genuine Christians, on average, to produce better moral fruit than non-Christians. Jesus himself said, "By your fruits you shall know them" (Matt. 7:16), but there are supporting premises that I doubt.

DAVID: Which ones?

TRENT: Well, I wonder how we know that Christians aren't morally superior to non-Christians. You can't make generalizations about an entire group of people from a few anecdotal encounters. The argument relies on a huge sociological claim that even one of the argument's major proponents, the philosopher Paul Draper, doubts we can prove.[39] There is even evidence to the contrary in that Christians tend to give more to charity.[40]

DAVID: Christians are more likely to give to their churches, not charity. That's not the same as giving to charity. The Church has a nice built-in system to milk believers and make them feel better about themselves, even though the money primarily goes to help the Church, not the poor.

TRENT: Actually, there is evidence that Christians give more to charities, and not just to their churches. But what's wrong with giving to the Church so that people can have access to the sacraments? After all, "man doesn't live by bread alone."

> If Christianity is true, then why aren't Christians noticeably more moral than non-Christians?

> How do we know that Christians aren't more virtuous than non-Christians?

How do
we explain
Christians
who are
jerks?

DAVID: Because it seems as though the sacraments aren't very effective. There are people who receive the Eucharist every week, but it doesn't seem to be doing them any good because they're still jerks Monday through Friday.

TRENT: This reminds me of when C.S. Lewis once compared the efficacy of Christianity to the cleaning power of a fictional brand of toothpaste called Whitesmile. Basically, he said you can't compare Frank who has naturally good teeth and doesn't use Whitesmile with Deborah who has habitual teeth problems and uses Whitesmile. We shouldn't compare believers and unbelievers who have different dispositions toward charity, but we should consider what a believer would be like if he had never been a Christian.[41]

DAVID: It's convenient for your argument that we can't directly observe the counterfactual of a Christian never having believed at all to see whether Christianity works or not. Also, Lewis is talking about isolated cases. The meager moral fruits argument asks us what the world would be like if God existed, and it makes a plausible case that Christians as a whole would be different from non-Christians, but in many cases, it's hard to tell them apart.

TRENT: Is it, though? Maybe if you consider moral fruits we all agree are good like following the Golden Rule or caring for the poor. But when you look at other moral issues, Christians clearly beat atheists and even many other religions. Consider abortion: the majority of weekly Mass-goers think it should be illegal, but the vast majority of atheists support legal abortion. The same is true for other evils like sexual activity outside marriage. You also see this kind of thing in the early Church, like in the second-century *Letter to Diognetus*, which says Christians "marry, as do all [others]; they beget children; but they do not destroy their offspring. They have a common table, but not a common bed. They are in the flesh, but they do not live after the flesh."

Why doesn't Christian opposition to evils like abortion and contraception demonstrate moral fruit?

DAVID: But it's easy to check a survey box and say you're against abortion. How many of those Christians actually help women experiencing unintended pregnancies?

TRENT: A lot of them donate money to crisis pregnancy centers and similar causes . . .

DAVID: They do that because those charities don't challenge them. It's a cause that makes them feel good about themselves. Why aren't more Christians donating to famine relief or to fight malaria?

TRENT: For some Christians, I think it's ignorance about either the scope of those problems or their ability to address them. Another problem is that you have people saying they're Catholic or Christian, but they don't really believe this, or they aren't living a grace-filled life.

DAVID: Ah, the *no true Scotsman fallacy*!

TRENT: Why do you say that?

DAVID: You're saying, "Christians are morally superior to non-Christians," and you can dismiss any counterexamples to that claim by saying they aren't "true Christians."

No True Scotsman Fallacy

"Not every one who says to me, 'Lord, Lord,' shall enter the kingdom of heaven, but he who does the will of my Father who is in heaven." (Matt. 7:21).

Occurs when someone makes a generalization that is refuted by a counterexample, and the defender of the generalization says the counterexample is not a true example of the rule in question. One example would involve positing Angus, a Scotsman who hates haggis (boiled sheep entrails), in order to falsify the claim that "every Scotsman loves haggis." The fallacy occurs if someone says without good reason that Angus is not a true Scotsman. David believes that Trent is committing the same fallacy by saying that only "true Christians" bear noticeable moral fruits.

TRENT: Although I admit that the class of "true Scotsman" might be an arbitrary distinction, the Bible clearly attests to there being true and false Christians. Now, I think anyone who is validly baptized is a Christian, but some of the baptized don't believe in the faith they profess. But that shouldn't cause us to doubt that there are genuine Christians whose actions make them distinct from the world.

DAVID: But if baptism really regenerates people, and the Eucharist lets them "feast on the body of Christ," then why doesn't every Catholic who has access to these sacraments demonstrate moral fruit?

TRENT: I think the answer to these questions is summarized in this famous principle from St. Thomas Aquinas that *grace does not destroy nature, but perfects it.*

CHAPTER 20

Meager Moral Fruits II

TRENT: Here's what I mean: God's grace doesn't trans-
form our souls in an extrinsic way that overpowers or
obliterates our natural habits and dispositions. Instead,
God's grace works *intrinsically* in our souls, elevating us
to the supernatural level of God's adopted children. But
though it does this, it does not automatically enable us
to *act* as God's children.

DAVID: So grace doesn't just make good works flow automatically from our being, is what you're saying?

TRENT: God's grace facilitates the natural desire to do
good and avoid evil. This means we have a responsibility
not just to say "yes" to God's initial offer of salvation—
we must continually say "yes" by allowing his grace to
operate in our souls and by developing natural virtues
through which God's grace can operate.

DAVID: So you're saying we can't merely compare Christians and non-Christians, since not every Christian will take advantage of the grace God makes available to him?

TRENT: Exactly. Consider a parallel case. Imagine someone saying, "We should doubt that healthy diets and exercise are good for you because the people who claim to eat well and exercise tend to be just as unhealthy as everyone else." You'd rightly point out that this doesn't take into account the many people who merely *claim* to do these things but don't actually follow their own advice. James 2:19 makes it clear there are beings—namely, demons—who believe that God exists *and* whose moral fruits are nothing but putrid poison.

DAVID: Christianity doesn't seem to be very effective, though, if so many believers fail to cooperate with God's grace and so only a few of them can really be called "true Christians."

TRENT: Even if the inconclusive sociological evidence did paint a bleak picture of American or Western Christians, that wouldn't be the end of it, since the class of *Christians* includes billions of people across space and time. In the fourth century, the Roman emperor Julian the Apostate griped about the superiority of Christian charity to what the government could provide its own citizens.

DAVID: Sounds like you guys could use a good old-fashioned persecution.

> "The moral virtues are acquired by human effort. They are the fruit and seed of morally good acts; they dispose all the powers of the human being for communion with divine love" (CCC 1804).

> We can't merely compare Christians and non-Christians, since not every Christian will take advantage of the grace God makes available to him.

TRENT: To be honest, the Christians that really prove the reality of grace today are those who live in extreme poverty, or under constant threat of execution by intolerant religious authorities, or both! It could also be the case that the absence of moral fruits is not the product of evil people, but the product of good saved people who profess only a kind of minimal morality. They live in a state of grace, but their holiness mostly comes in the form of what they don't do. They don't murder, commit adultery, swear, miss Mass, etc. But they also get so wrapped up in their lives that nobody ever says of them, "Wow, can you believe how much volunteering Catholic Mike does or how much Christian Cindy gives to the poor?"

"[Christians] support not only their own poor but ours as well; all men see that our people lack aid from us" (Julian the Apostate).

DAVID: Are you the "wrapped up Christian" who wishes he were "Catholic Mike"?

TRENT: Sometimes I feel that way. I feel like once I pour myself out to my wife, my children, the things that always need to be fixed around the house, and then to my work as an apologist, I feel as though I have nothing left.

DAVID: One could argue you're doing your charitable work by defending the Faith.

TRENT: That's an excuse I tell myself. "Hey, I spent eight hours today helping people better understand Jesus Christ through my writing and media, so I earned fifteen minutes playing my old Super Nintendo after the kids go to bed."

DAVID: It still works?

TRENT: Thirty years old and still going strong, my friend. But what about the Catholic who works at the widget factory and makes widgets all day and is way more tired than me? How can I blame him for being stuck on "the suburban treadmill" when I can't even model how to be a radical Christian in my own life?

DAVID: Apologist, heal thyself! In reality, though, it seems as if you don't think this is a refutation of *the* Faith, but a refutation of *your* faith. Christianity might still be plausible in the face of many mediocre believers, but you worry about the authenticity of your own faith.

TRENT: It's not a refutation of anything. It's more of an embarrassment. But it's not enough to make me give up my faith. It's a kick in the pants to be like the saints who demonstrate orchards of good moral fruit. And the fruit may not always be seen at a soup kitchen or on a mission field. But it can be in my living room with my smartphone in a drawer and my kids hearing a dramatic retelling of David and Goliath. It's present when I sow little seeds to help someone with an immortal soul be prepared to spend eternity with God.

DAVID: So do I get to be the Goliath in this case, and you're the David who slays me with a rock and then cuts off my head (the part that doesn't show up in kid's cartoons)?

TRENT: First, I tell my kids about the "rougher stuff" in the Bible when it is appropriate because I don't want them to have a crisis of faith if they discover that the Bible isn't a sanitized children's cartoon. Second, you aren't some kind of Philistine. You are an integral part of my intellectual life. You are the catfish to my cod.

DAVID: Come again?

TRENT: There's an old myth that when live cod were shipped in tanks across the ocean, the meat would be mushy because the codfish didn't swim very much. But when their natural predator, the catfish, was placed in the tank as well, they swam much more, and they were healthier as a result.

DAVID: I guess my job is to keep you on your toes without biting off your feet.

TRENT: I appreciate when you help me not to jump to illogical or false conclusions that are not essential to my faith. And you have brought up a lot of important questions I will think more deeply about. However, I think our dialogue should really be more of a "round-table discussion" that includes reason, religious experience, and the Holy Spirit.

DAVID: I don't know how I'll ever get a word in with those heavy hitters at the table!

TRENT: Don't kid yourself: lots of people have had someone like you at the table who ends up being the only person they end up listening to at the party. You are the wiliest of my "intellectual friends," but if I want to grow in wisdom, I shouldn't surround myself with a bunch of intellectual yes men. In fact . . .

DAVID: What?

TRENT: It's Laura and the kids. I hear them calling up to me from downstairs.

Go with God.

DAVID: So I guess we're done chatting?

TRENT: For now. I'm glad when you help me clarify things, but I can't talk with you forever. You'll always have concerning things to share with me, but as I quoted from Newman earlier, "ten thousand difficulties do not make a single doubt." There will always be time to puzzle over difficulties, but there won't always be time for the things that matter most in life.

DAVID: In that case, *vaya con Diós*—go with God.

TRENT: You too, old friend.

How to Handle Your Doubts

You may not face the same difficulties I do when I talk to my "inner skeptic." However, you probably face difficulties in your faith, so the principles I used when discussing difficulties with "David" may be helpful for times when you engage yours. I'd like to share those principles with you, along with a few others that didn't come up in my conversation with David.

1. RECOGNIZE DOUBT'S "HIDDEN FUEL"

Human beings are not strictly logical creatures. We often reach conclusions because of non-logical factors that affect us. One study found that judges were more likely to grant an inmate early parole if the case was heard early in the morning, or if the judge had recently taken a break (such as after lunch). A myriad of emotions and chemical processes in our bodies unconsciously influence us and can lead us to a false judgment or irrational conclusion.

If you're going to be thinking hard about our faith, make sure you've taken care of your body and mind. This includes maintaining a healthy diet, exercising, and balancing the use of technology (especially things that can become addictive like screens and social media). If your doubts coincide with enduring feelings of sadness or lethargy, you may want to speak to a competent Catholic therapist who can recommend treatment for an issue like clinical depression. Or such a person may be able to refer you to a spiritual director who can help you see that your doubt is actually a symptom of an unbalanced spiritual life. Catholic author Jennifer Fulwiler says,

> There was a time when I said I was experiencing doubts, but when I took a closer look I realized that it was simply a lack of consolation (i.e., a spiritual dry spell) rather than serious questions about the validity of the teachings of the Faith. "Doubt" is often used as a catch-all term that covers a variety of spiritual problems, so it's important to take a second look to make sure that you've diagnosed the situation correctly.

Along with taking care of your body and mind, above all else, you should make sure your soul is in good shape and in good friendship with God. This is why my second tip is identical to Fulwiler's second tip for dealing with doubt.

2. CONFESS YOUR SINS

Christian philosophers have noted that sin has a noetic effect on us—that is, it affects our mental faculties. Or in layman's terms, sin makes you stupid. St. Paul put it this way: "Although they knew God they did not honor him as God or give thanks to him, but they became futile in their thinking and their senseless minds were darkened" (Rom. 1:21).

Even if you don't feel as if you are struggling with any particular sin, the grace present in the sacrament of confession will help clear your mind and make it easier to be closer to God and better understand what he has revealed. The *Catechism* says,

> For those who receive the sacrament of penance with contrite heart and religious disposition, reconciliation "is usually followed by peace and serenity of conscience with strong spiritual consolation." Indeed the sacrament of reconciliation with God brings about a true "spiritual resurrection," restoration of the dignity and blessings of the life of the children of God, of which the most precious is friendship with God (1468).

In other cases, doubt can manifest itself as a way of trying to distance ourselves from God because of a desire (even an unconscious one) to avoid God's judgment. The Protestant pastor Timothy Keller once shared about how a fellow pastor he knew would engage college students who told him they were having doubts about their faith. He spoke to one young man for a while about scientific and historical objections to the Christian faith before asking him: whom have you been sleeping with? The student was shocked and asked in reply, "How did you know?"

But what about cases where a person feels physically and spiritually healthy, and what he is struggling with is an intellectual puzzle? How should they handle the "David," or the voice of doubt, that might pop into their heads?

3. SEPARATE DIFFICULTIES FROM DOUBTS

Some people conflate having difficulty understanding a truth of the Faith with doubting that truth and then think that if they doubt one truth of the Faith, perhaps they ought to doubt all of its truths. But a *difficulty* is not the same thing as a *doubt*. The former takes the form of keeping an open mind that curiously asks, "How *can* that be so?", whereas the latter represents a closed mind that says, "It *can't* be so!" Christians cannot doubt what God has revealed, but they might have difficulty understanding what he's revealed. To see the difference, let's compare the angel Gabriel's promises to Zechariah and Mary, telling both that they would have children—Zechariah with his wife, Mary with the miraculous help of the Holy Spirit.

Zechariah told the angel, "How shall I know this? For I am an old man, and my wife is advanced in years." As a priest serving in the Temple (Luke 1:5), Zechariah of all people should have known that God had the power to overcome the couple's infertility due to age, just as he had done for Abraham and Sarah centuries earlier (Gen. 17:15-16). Because Zechariah lacked humility and rashly concluded that God couldn't do this, Gabriel said, "You will be silent and unable to speak until the day that these things come to pass, because you did not believe my words, which will be fulfilled in their time" (Luke 1:20).

The story is different when Gabriel tells Mary she will

conceive a child. Mary replies, "How can this be, since I have no husband?" (v. 34). I should note that the Revised Standard Version, while being a good translation of the Bible, is faulty when it comes to this verse, since the Greek word for *husband* is not in it. Instead, a literal translation would be "How will this be since I know not man?" Here the word *know* is a euphemism for sexual intercourse. Even though Mary is betrothed to Joseph, she doesn't understand how she will have a child. This implies, as St. Augustine argued, that Mary had made a vow of virginity, and she was wed to Joseph so he could be her guardian in a patriarchal society.

Regardless, Mary's attitude is one of difficulty, not doubt. Whereas Zechariah *doubted* that God had the *power* to overcome his and his wife's infertility, Mary had *difficulty* understanding what *method* God would choose so that she would have a child. In response, Gabriel revealed the unprecedented method, saying "The Holy Spirit will come upon you, and the power of the Most High will overshadow you; therefore the child to be born will be called holy, the Son of God" (1:35).

If Mary can have difficulty understanding God's plan, even after an angel announces it to her, then there is nothing abnormal about us having difficulty understanding some aspects of our faith. The *Catechism* quotes Newman's famous saying, "Ten thousand difficulties do not make one doubt."

4. PUT DIFFICULTIES INTO PERSPECTIVE

Now that we understand that a healthy faith has room for difficulties, we should take stock of difficulties we struggle with and put them into perspective.

154 | Devil's Advocate

First, there are difficulties concerning things we would never expect to know or perfectly understand in this life. This might include what our unending life in heaven will be like, since St. Paul says of these realities, "For now we see in a mirror dimly, but then face to face. Now I know in part; then I shall understand fully" (1 Cor. 13:12).

Or it might relate to our understanding of God's attributes, such as how God can be timeless, or be immaterial, or create something from nothing. God is infinite, so "our human words always fall short of the mystery of God" (CCC 42), and we shouldn't expect our minds to understand the mystery of God's "inner life." But that doesn't disprove the solid reasons we have for believing that a timeless, immaterial God created the world from nothing.

In other words, we can experience the *wow* even if we can't grasp the *how*.

Another difficulty we wouldn't expect to resolve in this life relates to God's plan for our individual lives, especially when they involve suffering. The most difficult questions I have to answer as an apologist usually go like this: *why did God let this terrible thing happen to me or to someone I love?*

My honest answer is "I don't know."

Because God has infinite power and perfect knowledge, I know he can bring good from any evil and always make things right. But my tiny, finite mind can't even come close to explaining how God can do that in the face of certain evils. In those instances, I remember what the prophet Isaiah said, "For my thoughts are not your thoughts, neither are your ways my ways, says the Lord. For as the heavens are higher than the earth, so are my ways higher than your ways and my thoughts than your thoughts" (55:8-9).

Second, there are difficulties concerning issues that are not essential to our Faith. For example, some people may have difficulty accepting that certain miracles attributed to the saints or Marian apparitions really happened. But since the Church doesn't oblige us to believe in these events, any difficulty we have with them doesn't threaten the integrity of our faith as a whole.

Third, there are difficulties concerning issues of secondary importance for which the Church has not officially endorsed a particular answer. For example, the Church has not defined how one should interpret passages in Scripture that appear to describe God commanding the nation of Israel to kill the men, women, and even children among their enemies, the Canaanites. Theologians have proposed a variety of ways to interpret those passages, from literal commands that are justified based on God's sovereignty over human life to non-literal commands that were symbolic of totally rejecting Canaanite culture. (I survey these approaches in my book *Hard Sayings: A Catholic Approach to Answering Bible Difficulties*.)

In my conversation with David, you may have noticed that when he raised difficulties on secondary issues (like original sin), I offered several plausible explanations for those difficulties. Even if you're not sure how to resolve a difficulty like these, it won't prove that God does not exist or that Christianity isn't true. We have to balance the skepticism that might arise from a difficulty with a secondary issue against the confidence we have that comes from our faith in a foundational issue. That's why, when it comes to the "hard sayings" of Scripture, I told David that if I'm confident that God raised Jesus from the dead, and if Jesus believed that the Old Testament was inspired, then there must be a way to understand these texts that does not contradict God's perfect nature.

But what happens if we have difficulties with doctrines that are foundational to our faith? This might include the existence of God, the Incarnation, or the Real Presence of Christ in the Eucharist. These are the most serious difficulties, as they can quickly lead to doubt and then a complete rejection of our faith. Here are some ways a person can approach difficulties with these doctrines:

- Remember that there is a difference between knowing that these doctrines are true and showing they are true. If you are faced with an objection you feel unable to answer, that in itself should not necessarily be a cause for doubt. An innocent man may be unable to prove his innocence in a court of law, but that by itself doesn't mean he has to give up his personal belief in his innocence. You can know that something is true (including our Catholic faith) even if you can't show that it is true to other people.

- Accept the limits of your own knowledge. Just because you may not be able to answer an objection or question about our faith, it doesn't follow that no one else in the 2,000-year history of the Church has likewise failed to respond to such a challenge. Prayerfully consider what the Magisterium has said on these issues as well as theologians and apologists who have studied it.

- Don't think the grass is greener on the other side. When David raised the prospect of abandoning the Faith in order to have peace through another belief system, I pointed out that the only way to have a belief system that doesn't face *any* difficulties is simply not to think very hard about it. For example, even if one abandons God because of the problem of evil, the problem of evil remains. The pain of suffering doesn't change, but now the hope of redeeming it is gone, and questions about how to reconcile evil with God get replaced with questions about how to reconcile things like objective good and evil with a purposeless, accidental universe.

5. IF YOU'RE ON THE FENCE, CONSIDER TAKING PASCAL'S WAGER

What happens if a foundational difficulty has caused you so much confusion that you aren't even sure our faith is true anymore? If this happens, you should resist the temptation to gauge our faithfulness based on how much we *feel* that our faith is true. If you feel as if you are genuinely on the fence, yet you want Catholicism to be true and it feels as though your heart just isn't in it anymore, then consider taking *Pascal's Wager*.

In his work *Pensées*, a French word for "thoughts," Blaise Pascal puts forward arguments for the existence of God but doesn't consider any of them decisive to an undecided person. He then offers this advice:

> To which side shall we incline? Reason can
> decide nothing here. There is an infinite chaos
> which separated us. A game is being played at
> the extremity of this infinite distance where
> heads or tails will turn up. What will you wa-
> ger? . . . Let us weigh the gain and the loss in
> wagering that God is. Let us estimate these two
> chances. If you gain, you gain all; if you lose,
> you lose nothing. Wager, then, without hesita-
> tion that he is.

Many people misunderstand the wager as being an argument about avoiding hell. They think Pascal is saying,
"Believe in God, because if you're right, you get heaven,
and if you're wrong, you'll never know, because you won't
survive your own death. But if you don't believe in God,
then you'll never know you were right, and if you're
wrong, you'll be damned for all eternity."

Hell didn't feature into Pascal's argument, and this is
helpful for addressing an objection to the wager called
the *wrong hell problem*. Namely, what if God punishes me
with hell for choosing the wrong religion? Instead, Pascal's wager says it is worthwhile to believe in God because
you'll experience the happiness of following God not just
in eternal life, but also in this life. You have everything
to gain when it comes to believing in God and nothing
comparable to gain when it comes to disbelieving in God.
In fact, a recent Pew study has shown that in the United
States, thirty-six percent of actively religious people say
they are "very happy" compared to twenty-five percent of
religiously unaffiliated people.[42]

The wager can also be applied to the debate over Catholicism and Protestantism. I've met some Protestants who have said they wish Catholicism were true. I tell them, "Well, why not go to Mass and at least act as if it's true, and see what happens to you?"

Finally, no matter what happens, pray and stay close to God. Even if you feel as if God is far away or doesn't even exist, don't stop praying to God. Don't turn away from Catholic friends, but find ones (or a spiritual director, if you can) who will peacefully accompany your journey and patiently listen to your concerns. Spend time with our Lord in an adoration chapel. Even if you think you are looking at just a piece of bread, take a moment to still your heart and just listen. Don't expect God to appear as a burning bush to resolve every doubt, but spend time, lots of time, praying, listening, reading, and receiving the wisdom God gave in Psalm 46:10: "Be still and know that I am God."

I can't give you a perfect answer for your doubts, but know that I have said a prayer for you, and for anyone struggling with his faith who is reading this book. Even if you don't believe it, or can't accept evidence for it, God loves you and wants you to live in his love forever. As a result, if you genuinely cannot make up your mind on an issue (for example, does God exist? is Catholicism true?), then there is no harm in a kind of "play-acting" that lives out the Catholic faith one would want to be true. C.S. Lewis said something similar in that even if a person doesn't feel as though he can accept Christianity, if he just chooses to live like a Christian, eventually, his heart can catch up to his will.

I'll leave you with Lewis's words, since he struggled with difficulties after the death of his wife, but he did not let those difficulties nullify his faith. He said:

> When you are not feeling particularly friendly but know you ought to be, the best thing you can do, very often, is to put on a friendly manner and behave as if you were a nicer person than you actually are. And in a few minutes, as we have all noticed, you will be really feeling friendlier than you were. Very often the only way to get a quality in reality is to start behaving as if you had it already. . . . Now, the moment you realize "Here I am, dressing up as Christ," it is extremely likely that you will see at once some way in which at that very moment the pretense could be made less of a pretense and more of a reality.[43]

Endnotes

1 "C.S. Lewis on Heaven, Earth and Outer Space," *Decision Magazine*, September 1963.

2 "Consciousness is just another physical process. So it has as much trouble producing aboutness as any other physical process. . . . It's got to be an illusion, since nothing physical can be about anything. . . . The clumps of matter that constitute your conscious thoughts can't be about stuff either." Alex Rosenberg, *The Atheist's Guide to Reality: Enjoying Life without Illusions* (W.W. Norton & Company: New York, 2011), 193.

3 "When John 21:15-17 is tied to the common Roman Catholic exegesis of Matthew 16:16-19, the argument gains a certain plausibility." D.A. Carson, *The Gospel according to John* (Grand Rapids, MI: Wm. B. Eerdmans, 1991), 678.

4 This has come from conversations with the Real Atheology team, one member of whom I debated in Houston in 2021. Consider also these words from atheist Graham Oppy: "Perhaps its [sic] worth thinking here about the official theology of the Catholic Church, i.e. about the best developed version of traditional Western theology. This theology has been worked on by countless extremely intelligent people over a period of nearly 2000 years." Graham Oppy, "Review of: J.P. Moreland (ed.) The Creation Hypothesis" (Downers Grove, IL: InterVarsity Press), Internet Infidels (1998). Available online at https://infidels.org/library/modern/graham-oppy-review-m.

5 See *Summa Theologiae* I:7:4 and Richard Cartwright, "Aquinas on Infinite Multitudes," *Medieval Philosophy and Theology,* 6 (1997), 183-201.

161

---

6 A variant of this argument is proposed in Michael Murray, *Nature Red in Tooth and Claw: Theism and the Problem of Animal Suffering* (Oxford: Oxford University Press, 2008).

7 While he doesn't promote suicide, it's not hard to see how one might reach that conclusion by reading David Benatar's 2008 book *Better Never to Have Been: The Harm of Coming into Existence.*

8 Metropolitan Hierotheos (Vlachos) of Nafpaktos, "Life After Death." "Publications of the Holy Monastery of the Nativity of the Virgin Mary (Pelagia)," February 1, 2009. See also Ioannes Polemes, *Theophanes of Nicaea: His Life and Works*, vol. 20 (Verlag der Österreichischen Akademie der Wissenschaften, 1996), 99. "Paradise and hell exist not in the form of a threat and a punishment on the part of God but in the form of an illness and a cure. Those who are cured and those who are purified experience the illuminating energy of divine grace, while the uncured and ill experience the caustic energy of God" (Fr. Christopher Klitou, http://www.christopherklitou.com/ask_an_orthodox_priest_question_36.htm).

9 C.S. Lewis, *The Great Divorce* (New York: Harper One, 2009), Kindle edition.

10 Sam Harris, "10 myths—and 10 truths—about atheism," *Los Angeles Times* (December 24, 2006).

11 "Scientists and Belief," Pew Research Center (November 5, 2009). Available online at https://www.pewforum.org/2009/11/05/scientists-and-belief.

12 For more, see Elaine Ecklund, *Science vs. Religion: What Scientists Really Think* (New York: Oxford University Press, 2010).

13 This can be seen at the 2020 Philosophy Papers Survey (PhilPapers Survey), edited by David Bourget (Western University) and David Chalmers (New York University). Available online at https://survey2020.philpeople.org.

14 Peter Atterton, "A God Problem," *The New York Times* (March 25, 2019)

15 The Protestant philosopher Alvin Plantinga made a similar observation of Richard Dawkins's book *The God Delusion*. He wrote: "Now despite the fact that this book is mainly philosophy, Dawkins is not a philosopher (he's a biologist). Even taking this into account, however, much

of the philosophy he purveys is at best jejune. You might say that some of his forays into philosophy are at best sophomoric, but that would be unfair to sophomores; the fact is [grade inflation aside], many of his arguments would receive a failing grade in a sophomore philosophy class. This, combined with the arrogant, smarter-than-thou tone of the book, can be annoying." Alvin Plantinga, "The Dawkins Confusion," *Books and Culture* (2007). Available online at https://www.booksandculture.com/articles/2007/marapr/1.21.html.

16 See The 2020 PhilPapers Survey, eds. David Bourget and David Chalmers, available online at https://survey2020.philpeople.org.

17 See David Lewis, *On the Plurality of Worlds* (Oxford: Blackwell Publishers, 1986).

18 This criticism has also been noted in Edward Feser's book *The Last Superstition: A Refutation of the New Atheism* (2010).

19 See for example Edward Feser, *Five Proofs of the Existence of God* (San Francisco: Ignatius Press, 2017), 9.

20 Joseph Bergeron and Gary Habermas, "The Resurrection of Jesus: A Clinical Review of Psychiatric Hypotheses for the Biblical Story of Easter" (1973-2015) *Liberty Baptist Theological Seminary* (2015). Available online at: https://digitalcommons.liberty.edu/lts_fac_pubs/402/.

21 This claim can be found in Robert M. Price's, *Beyond Born Again: Toward Evangelical Maturity* (Eugene, OR: Apocryphal Books, 1993), 67.

22 Vincent Bugliosi with Curt Gentry, *Helter Skelter: The True Story of the Manson Murders* (W.W. Norton & Company, 1994), 466.

23 See Sadeh, et al. "Postictal blindness in adults," *Journal of Neurology, Neurosurgery, and Psychiatry*, no. 46 (1983), 566-569.

24 See Todd Compton. *In Sacred Loneliness: The Plural Wives of Joseph Smith* (Signature Books, 1997).

25 Pliny, *Letters* 10.97.

26 Cowdery and Harris temporarily left Mormonism and then returned to that faith, seeking rebaptism. David Whitmer never returned to Mormonism but ordained his nephew in the Church of Christ in a denomination now known as the "Whitmerites".

27 Mike Licona, *The Resurrection of Jesus: A New Historiographical Approach* (Downer's Grove, IL: IVP Academic, 2010), 491.

28 D.A. Carson, "Matthew", in *The Expositor's Bible Commentary*, vol. 8, ed. Frank E. Gaebelein (Grand Rapids, MI: Zondervan, 1984), 368.

29 "Eucharistic teaching, it should be understood at the outset, was in general unquestioningly realist, i.e., the consecrated bread and wine were taken to be, and were treated and designated as, the Savior's body and blood." J.N.D. Kelly, *Early Christian Doctrines*, 5th ed. (New York: Bloomsbury Academic, 2000), 198.

30 St. Augustine, *Against the Fundamental Epistle of Manichaeus*, 5.

31 Alphonsus de Liguori, *The Glories of Mary* (London: Burns and Oates, 1868), 112.

32 Ibid.

33 Diarmaid MacCulloch. *All Things Made New: The Reformation and Its Legacy* (New York: Oxford University Press, 2016), Kindle edition.

34 Holweck, Frederick. "Immaculate Conception." The Catholic Encyclopedia. Vol. 7. New York: Robert Appleton Company, 1910. November 16, 2021.

35 Tim Perry, *Mary for Evangelicals: Toward an Understanding of the Mother of Our Lord* (Downers Grove, IL: InterVarsity Press, 2006), 113.

36 On November 12, 1950, Pope Pius XII solemnly declared and defined that "the Immaculate Mother of God, the ever Virgin Mary, having completed the course of her earthly life, was assumed body and soul into heavenly glory." The phrase "having completed the course of her earthly life" leaves open the possibility that Mary was assumed into heaven after death, or that she was assumed alive into heaven (which is the minority view among theologians).

37 See Milton Friedman, "A Friedman doctrine: The Social Responsibility of Business Is to Increase Its Profits," *The New York Times* (September 13, 1970).

38 Daniel Silliman and Kate Shellnutt, "Ravi Zacharias Hid Hundreds of Pictures of Women, Abuse During Massages, and a Rape Allegation," *Christianity Today*, February 11, 2021.

39 Jeffrey Jay Lowder, "Are Christians the Best Argument Against

Christianity?", *The Secular Outpost* (August 6, 2012).

40 Alex Daniels, "Religious Americans Give More, New Study Finds," The Chronicle of Philanthropy (November 25, 2013).

41 C.S. Lewis, *Mere Christianity* (New York: Harper Collins, 1952), 208.

42 You find this same "happiness gap" in many other countries, including Japan, Germany, Peru, and Australia ("Are religious people happier, healthier?", 2019, https://www.pewresearch.org/fact-tank/2019/01/31/are-religious-people-happier-healthier-our-new-global-study-explores-this-question).

43 *Mere Christianity*, 162.

About the Author

After his conversion to the Catholic faith, Trent Horn earned master's degrees in the fields of theology, philosophy, and bioethics. He serves as a staff apologist for Catholic Answers, where he specializes in teaching Catholics to graciously and persuasively engage those who disagree with them. Trent models that approach each week on the radio program *Catholic Answers Live* and on his own podcast, *The Counsel of Trent*. He has also been invited to debate at UC Berkeley, UC Santa Barbara, and Stanford University. Trent is an adjunct professor of apologetics at Holy Apostles College, has written for *The National Catholic Bioethics Quarterly*, and is the author of nine books, including *Answering Atheism*, *The Case for Catholicism*, and *Why We're Catholic: Our Reasons for Faith, Hope, and Love*.